C000138301

DUJON WALSHAM

SELF-MOTIVATION:

Anyone can do IT if I did IT

First published in Great Britain as a softback original in 2019

Copyright © Dujon Walsham

The moral right of this author has been asserted.

Typeset in Palatino

Editing, design, typesetting and publishing by UK Book Publishing

www.ukbookpublishing.com

ISBN: 978-1-913179-19-9

SELF-MOTIVATION:

Anyone can do IT if I did IT

CHAPTER 1
– WHAT IS SELF-MOTIVATION

S elf-Motivation? Couldn't tell you its real definition that everybody would agree with, but my story will provide an interpretation of how I see it.

It could come from literally… anywhere! For me, any and everywhere topped with various events and points later on explained in this journey.

I still remember the times when I was still in school where you don't really have an idea of what you would want to do when you are older…at least not a definitive one. I had dabbled in many pies of ideas which I wanted to fulfil – for example, one of the things I had an early thought of was becoming an author. I had (and still have) a very vivid imagination which has contributed to getting me where I am today…but also to enhance my ideas and chance taking.

The Author In Me

My very first type of structured hobby was to write books and stories. I was obsessed with getting notepads and book type diaries, and literally just freestyled an entire story with characters, plots, beginning, middle and ends. As this was the normal structure of how to plan to write an actual book, for me it was just too slow. The moment I started to formulate a plan for a book I eventually gave up; it just wasn't fun for me to have an actual plan or synopsis for an idea of a fictional story I just wanted to let the story write itself.

The soul of writing for me came from the ink shedding from a fountain pen, and was really about the perfect pen. Fountain pens where I could get ink cartridges to refill them, vintage fountain pens – the fancier they looked the more motivated I felt to create a great story.

At school where some of the tasks or homework assignments were to write a story, normally based on something we had already watched, read or about mythological continuations, I could really write pages beyond pages beyond pages. Grades wise was very good as I really came alive from doing this.

Another important part of the writing ritual for me...the perfect handwriting. The old style writing with everything slanted that was really my thing and I had to know how to master that at all costs.

The first book that ever came from me when I was eleven was a book called "Day of the Flood", and it really was inspired from a computer game I used to have on the Sega Saturn games console called "Guardian Heroes". The relationship between them? None whatsoever! Just the storyline grips just inspired something completely different.

The Somewhat business side of me

Such ideas I had when I was younger had me so dedicated to the point that regular procedures of schooling got put on the side-lines.

For example, in Primary school I had come up with the idea of wanting to create the very first newsletter that the school had ever seen. I was so dedicated to bringing life to this, one time I came into the classroom about half way in the middle of class, whilst it was still going on and everyone's head including teachers and teaching assistants turned around. But instead of me taking the normal route to sit with the rest of the children...nope! I went to the opposite part of the classroom altogether, with the prints I had, grabbed a stapler and started creating a table of contents and stapling the correct pages together.

I don't think anyone knew what to think at the time but I remember the teacher waiting for about a minute, which in actuality is a long time for a child to roam free school wise without anything being said to them.

"Dujon?"

"Yes?"

"Are you going to join the rest of the class?"

So I put everything down and went back to the group of children.

When I look back at this time just thinking to myself what in the world possessed me to just be locked and zoned in to an idea like that to the point I just came into the classroom nonchalantly and ignored the class being taught to do a newsletter...

Some motivations just couldn't be explained at this point. A natural determination to want something achieved at any cost? Zoning attention that should be dedicated to getting a mandatory education to formulate an idea I randomly had?

Maybe this was an early indication of still having your child like drivers of where you have that keen interest and ideology to do anything and everything and learn from it.

Another idea of what I thought I wanted to do was to trade in the stock market. What sparked this? An obvious thing in everyone's mind would of course be money and this is partly true but not 100% motivation for me.

Just the aspect of the stocks going up and down in price held a fascination for me and the first thing for me to do was to explore it but in a different way altogether.

For example I used to be quite a hardcore gamer...hardcore to the point where if I won at something the response would be "yeah ok well he lives and breathes this" and if they beat me it would be almost like beating Floyd Mayweather to them. But what I picked up on when I became of age was to collect vintage games, games which I had used to own a decade ago when I was much smaller which started off being more of a nostalgic trip. There was an interesting edge to it for me because there was a lot of sentimental value in them as I had great memories triggered from them as well as great markers in points of my life.

So I used to analyse the prices of the games ensuring I could get them at the lowest prices that I possibly could – of course at the same time these easily cost the same price as up to date games of my time and indeed far exceeding them too.

Eventually I had a huge collection of games which had been maintained for several years, in alphabetical order and each individually wrapped so that they didn't get any dust. Eventually I had seen that a lot of them had seriously surged in price and rarity, and I had then decided to sell them on (which I had done several times over the years!) and actually made a great profit ranging between three to four times more than what I had initially purchased them for, which was huge – but for me I didn't really look at it like that, but more the indication of growing education on how stocks somewhat worked.

The point is that motivation can really be picked up from anywhere, anything, everywhere and everything. Everyone operates differently and perceives differently.

My vocabulary grew extensively from the uncanniest type of ways, just watching cartoons and shows on Nickelodeon (showing my age here). My dad had taken me to a private type of library or school as such for whatever reason, where I was given a comprehension test of some sort. I wasn't actually sure of what the purpose was but maybe it was done just to gauge what level they felt I may be at, good baseline prep for me for either secondary school and further on. I would have been about ten years old at the time.

So on this test they had words which I wouldn't even think would be on a test for someone my age like "What is the meaning of Conflagration?" which I answered literally in seconds saying "that means fire".

Everyone (well, two people: the test person and my dad) just looked at me strangely, saying "How do you even know that?"

I replied, "I learned it on Sister Sister."

So it's just amazing where you can adapt and pick up things from and this had stuck with me ever since.

They thought they would be more slicker and hit me with something else such as "Can you spell the word rambunctious and give me its definition" – again the exact same story and at this point they were looking at me even more confused. Mainly because though my dad was setting me homework to step up my own knowledge, these were things that were never told or taught to me from him.

Again: "How do you even know that?"

I replied, "Learnt it on Kenan and Kel!"

I'm not born with any type of special gift that makes me stand out from anybody, I didn't exactly go to the greatest of schools in every case so there was no special teaching I had received, so I feel anybody is more than capable of unlocking their true potential regardless.

If I possess any type of attribute which some would consider an "edge" of some sort it's that I'm normally quiet, don't speak a lot...

at all. So maybe this perhaps tunes up more of the other senses like sight and listening, which can be investigated later on in this journey.

But again this is not something which anybody else is incapable of doing, not everything a successful person does would work for you just because they are successful, they could be wrong, they could be right; it doesn't matter because you can only go far when you stick to being you...of course if you have any attributes which may alienate you from success then do please change them with immediate effect.

Remember this...perfection is a soulless goal. A lot of people say they are a perfectionist which is great from a behaviour standpoint, but nothing can really ever be perfect...just perfect for you.

Something that's perfect doesn't really have a soul, the imperfections of it show you and your creativity, your stamp and your brand and you only really make it perfect...for you.

CHAPTER 2
– BIRTH OF INDEPENDENCE

I had decided at some point during secondary school that I wanted to further pursue the Information Technology side. At first I was apprehensive about this route because I was so into computers that what I didn't want to possibly do was turn a hobby into a future job I didn't like and that would actually feel like a job. Sometimes what you are passionate about as a hobby can often become materialized and the honeymoon period ends extremely quickly, so when you do make that decision of carrying something you are passionate for across, ensure that it doesn't become a chore, but still remains a hobby, still something you enjoy that always breathes life.

Sometimes you can love doing what you do for fun but when it comes to taking it more seriously and into a possible profession...it stops being fun. But I had decided to take that risk.

I had taken IT classes which I had done in secondary school but this covered absolutely nowhere near what I wanted to be involved in, it was mainly more to do with how to use office applications as opposed to the actual technical structure of a computer and much more beyond my imagination at this point. My motivation for this was in parallel with the grades I had achieved for it – I don't remember the exact grade but I can assure you it was not an F, but still not a great a letter in the alphabet.

But it didn't matter to me, because as far as I was concerned I knew exactly what I wanted to do and I knew exactly what I wanted to learn and it just wasn't going to happen at secondary school for me.

So then the next route was college; not an easy ride to find one with any spaces but I managed to squeeze into one not too long after my birthday.

My experience there was a little better in terms of what I wanted to cover, but overall it was still quite theory based. And this is a side note really of that: if you feel that you are not getting what you want out of something then you can always build on that thirst for knowledge of anything elsewhere...more importantly at home and it costs absolutely nothing. But sometimes these thoughts don't always click like that – when you are young, you just simply see the options you have in front of you, but a very select few have the thought process of doing just that. At this point I didn't think like that until maybe a year or so later, so it's commendable for anybody that did or does think like this at the age I was then, or even younger.

During this time there was a girl I had dated quite briefly...but she may have been one of the first real influences I've seen in terms of work ethic outside of my mother and other random areas that I would obtain knowledge from. When it was time for any kind of coursework, homework, any work as a matter of fact, not only was it done at a high quality level but it was done pretty damn quickly and it never really hit me until later on, thinking "how does she even do this?".

Also she would provide at least five and up to ten additional pieces of work on each of them which would only propel her grades up, which was really impressive and even more in retrospect. I was amazed by this at the time too, but at the same time I may have been a little bit too ignorant in my way of thinking to put in the same amount of effort because I was still adamant that though I was getting better information than I did at secondary school, it still was not enough compared to what I wanted.

As time went by it was then announced the course had actually ran out of money, not something I've ever heard before coming from a college, but that was the situation, so the first year was all we had. I really didn't have time to process what I was going to do next

(*Self-Motivation Point: always expect the unexpected. You will never be prepared for every situation so it's always important to stay on your toes.*)

And after the amount of time it took just to get this placement in college it wasn't a journey I was prepared to take as a position at the college had to be created due to lack of space and so many colleges had given me the run around stating there were places and coming to find out there wasn't. So, my mum and I looked around for courses around business management as I wanted to head in a direction where I could lean right into work experience and eventually a job. I had come across some business course and job role in the same college which had really caught my eye. I believe it was paying £150 a week at the time and for me that was like hearing £1500 a week! Especially at the time when I was supposed to be getting £30 a week from EMA that never came until we had to chase it to get a big delayed payment, but that's different story.

Also at this time I had a job on the weekend on a Sunday as a market trader selling music CDs, which was a long ten-hour day for £10, but at the time that £10 was so worth it for me and I had been working there from when I was 15-16 years old, so secondary school times with £10 was huge for me (actually it meant KFC for dinner but still huge nonetheless).

Now I'm pursuing the business course which required me to undergo an evaluation test to get through the first round before you proceed to the interview, which was a round of English and maths slightly above GCSE level. Later in that week I had the confirmation that I had passed and an interview as arranged for me at the college.

Now here we are...my very first interview ever for a paid job role. I was about 17 at the time.

I really had no expectations for myself or for what was to come.

(*Self-Motivation point: When you have no expectations you almost have no nerves. If you set an expectation the nerves will hit you hard. The greatest results can come from when you don't set criteria of success or failure, the success is really that you are grabbing an opportunity and going for it.*)

So I attended the interview; there were about three interviewers on the panel but I didn't let it faze me at all, and I really did a remarkable job, in fact I did something which you wouldn't do in an interview, especially your first one, which was to be 100% honest. Not to suggest that a majority lie, but when you are competing against others the urge to over-embellish your own skills and experience, especially when you are on the come up, it does come somewhat naturally, just the competitor in us commands this.

Now bear in mind my motivation was selective to what I wanted to accomplish, and because I felt what I was learning in college and secondary school were not cutting it for me, it reflected in my grades, and I went on to explain this in the interview, and when I say honest I meant in addressing why my grades may not have reflected the motivation I displayed and explained that this opportunity was to prove to myself and them what I was truly capable of. And I really did perform well with as much energy as you can imagine from a 17 year old hunting for his first role and first actual structured pay.

A few days had past. Even though I initially had no expectations I thought to myself I had this in the bag.

So I got the call and was told:

"Brilliant interview. But unfortunately, it's a no."

I wasn't really upset about it, but the same time I was confused thinking isn't this a contradiction? What's the point of it being a brilliant interview if I didn't get the job?

I don't really remember what the reason was as I wasn't really told, I felt it may have been down to the grades I had which could have been better, but out of shock I don't think I speculated as to why as much, or even ask as to why for that matter.

I sat on it for a couple of days and then it eventually came up in conversation with my mum like "Yeah they said no".

"Did they give a reason as to why you didn't get the role?" she asked.

I said no they didn't.

She didn't exactly take it well, so one of the first things she did was get on the phone and ask me for the name of the person who had interviewed me.

She wanted to find out exactly what the feedback was because she was driven by the fact I was told I didn't get the role after giving a brilliant interview and no feedback or reasoning as to why I didn't get the job, as otherwise I wouldn't know what to work on or brush up on.

The person had responded that it was down to my "age".

This was where the conversation got a bit more intense, because my age couldn't have been a great excuse when they knew it from the beginning, so my mum proceeded to challenge this with not much of a response, so the guy who interviewed me opted for a referral for another avenue, which eventually led to a dead-end. Time and time we would face obstacles but I was resilient to keep on trying.

CHAPTER 3
– OBSERVING

G oing back to the drawing board, I had gone back to the college where I had originally done the double A-Level IT course thinking let's just see what happens here and what is available. That's when I had discovered that all students who had been on the first IT course could migrate over to a new one that had opened which was the BTEC IT course for a 3 year semester.

At this point I guess I was more relieved that there was an option to just get back into the swing of having a route I could go through, but I still wasn't satisfied. Until, that is, we had a specific class where there was this teacher... who just captured me with almost exactly what I wanted to learn about. The real technical stuff, so technical they were things I had never even heard of before. And that's when all the motivation started flooding back again – finally there was a glimmer of hope, something real I could develop on.

To put it quite simply, this was the only class and teacher that had made the BTEC course remotely interesting as at this time every single class was getting cancelled left, right and centre and we just had 3-4 hour breaks in between.

Great for my lazy side but very counterproductive.

One time me and a few other class-mates went up to the library, could only assume we were studying but with so many classes being cancelled I would say we were just hanging out until the next class was to commence in 5 hours' time.

One of the teachers had walked past and had engaged us in conversation as we were talking about what we wanted to do workwise in IT, so some of them had asked pressure like questions to the teacher asking "if we complete this course would we be able to get a job in the IT industry?". And the response was literally no answer, that and a lot of muddled up words which didn't really answer anything. And that's when I really had the revelation I had always known in the back of my mind. If the teachers didn't even have any faith of our future from doing a course in the same industry we wanted to work in, then what chance did we have? And just like I said my grades reflected my motivation, whilst the cancelled classes reflected theirs as well.

So I decided to do something about it, and as soon as I got home I started looking at all kinds of institutes that focused specifically on IT courses, anything which would provide a better route or option than what I already had. I didn't have too much knowledge as to what I was looking for but my determination wouldn't let me stop. Then I found something, it was some kind of advanced college or academy of some sort which had industry type IT courses with industry recognized certifications and it had official Microsoft approval stamps all over it.

"That's it!" I said. So I filled out the form with my contact details as a stab in the dark to see where it would go and that was me done for the night.

Next morning my mum woke me up and said, "Microsoft are on the phone for you."

"Microsoft?" I said while I was trying to wake up. Then I was like oh right...the form I did last night. I took the call to see what was going to happen and they were interested in visiting us where we lived so I thought of a suitable time to come, until I was being challenged again by my mum like "Who are these people! What do they want with my son! And what they want to come here for!"

So whilst I explained what the deal was she understood and was keen on the idea.

Later on the representative came, and I guess I had no expectations at this point, I really didn't know what was going to happen. But after speaking briefly he explained about all of these industry courses, exams and certifications that I had never heard before.

Things like A+, MCSE (Microsoft Certified Systems Engineer), Cisco CCNA (Cisco Certified Network Associate), CCIE (Cisco Certified Internetwork Expert) etc and what kind of information was covered in each. Now we were getting some interest now, but what really caught my eye was the average salary for having any of these certifications, which were starting from approximately £18,000 to up to £50,000 a year.

For someone about to turn 18 they were insane salaries. I mean £50,000 a year!? Yes! I wanted the knowledge to be able to at least get a career, but for a salary that size too it sounded too good to be true, but my own research proved this to be not far from reality.

Of course these options weren't just going to be given to us, as these were private courses. And they had a hefty tag on themselves – I guess this is the part you're glad you're in a privileged position where you are glad you aren't the parent in this scenario. But even I could see the struggle in even being able to remotely afford anything like that. So once we wrapped up the evening, the idea of paying something like £10,000 for all of those courses wasn't really realistic, but now I had a name for these courses, a route, something I could look into myself.

Later on that evening my dad had come to visit, but at the time his visit wasn't really enthusiastic because prior to the meeting we had told him about this appointment, the time and what was going to transpire. But he quickly denounced and removed himself from it thinking we wanted him to pay for it saying "well you know I can't do anything, I can't do anything".

What he failed to understand, was that we wanted him as adult/parental and moral support. We had no intention of just going for a ridiculous (at the time) priced private course, but just to listen, but then at the same time it was probably for the best he didn't show as who knows how that could have turned out with further added scepticism.

So, after showing up, we spoke briefly about the courses, training and potential and handed him a piece of paper which detailed the industry standard courses, exams and the salaries attached to them.

He looked at it for 10 seconds, threw it to the side and said, "No, that's ridiculous there is no way you can earn that much from doing that course, waste of time, it's garbage."

At first I thought it couldn't have been a more negative ignorant response...but at the same time who wouldn't have been a bit sceptical about it without any prior knowledge. But this really lit a fire in me to prove anyone that thought this was ridiculous to be wrong.

(*Self-Motivation Point:* *Adversity and doubt can be huge drivers in motivation so that you can prove to yourself that you can do it and it can be done. But also more to the point of achieving it for yourself rather than to do it just to prove others wrong.*)

Next morning, I was getting ready for college and my mum called me to her room and said with a concerned look. "I know you want to do that course, but I simply just can't afford it, I'm really sorry."

To be honest I didn't even expect for her to try and pull off something like that; as young and as driven as I was to do it, I knew it was an insane price back then so it didn't matter much to me. Because now

I had something to build from, so it helped me persevere with the BTEC course a while longer.

My ambition to do these exams and courses was then again met by more sceptics, but this time also laughter. I told some of the classmates at college about it, and they just laughed in my face, hard, hysterically and even tried to break down every logic as to why it was stupid. But I was not backing down in any way! I envisaged myself doing it and in my mind I was doing it right now. What makes this entire story (back then and till up to this day) is that they were the same ones who started the conversation with one of the teachers about can we get a career from this, but my idea was just met with pure laughter. Again I was going to show everyone that this can be done.

About a couple of weeks later with the classmates kind of putting up with my talks about these courses, we had a class which normally got cancelled every time we were due for it. As a matter of fact, I think it was a teacher we had seen in my last double A level course that ran out of money. But anyway, when this class did take place (3 times in total of 3-4 months) we would do nothing but just talk, play music and mess around, pretty much anything that didn't involve listening to the teacher.

Then my classmates drummed up the same conversation again and asked the teacher, "Can we get a job after this?" She said "No! Not unless you get specific IT courses that are industry recognized like... A+ for example."

That literally stopped everything for me and now I was all ears hearing that, and I asked, "You know about those?"

"Yes, some guys come here to take these exams in one of our classrooms as a testing centre. They are expensive but they are very heavy in their careers."

I couldn't believe my ears. This teacher, I probably saw her twice, and she came out with everything I had researched that everyone was laughing at me for, and a rare appearance from this teacher to shed light on what I had been saying already – this had to be some kind of sign.

But my classmates still weren't paying attention at all. And they made the conversation up again! And still thought it was ridiculous!?

Sometimes telling someone you are going to do something that will achieve such and such means absolutely nothing to sceptics. They will only engage once they see the end result. They don't want to hear you bought an Aston Martin – why would I believe that you aren't special in any way etc? You sometimes have to drive up in one in order for them to pay attention. From that day on I knew there was no going back.

So the next morning I had a game plan, my mission was simple: I was going to do this by any means by infiltrating the best options.

Now I knew I would meet resistance where my mum was concerned, but I absolutely did not care; even my dad would have got the same talking to and nobody was convincing me to go back to college, not after that revelation. The fire was lit, it was time.

So it was about 9 or 10am and she was like: "Aren't you going to college?"

And I was ready for it and said, "Nope. I'm not doing this course no more I'm done."

She was like: "What!? You better get your things ready now, I'm not playing."

And I said, "Neither am I. I'm not doing this no more. Going to a course where every class gets cancelled and learning nothing. I want those Industry courses and exams. I heard a teacher tell all of us we can't get no jobs from this. So why am I going to commit to a 3 year course, get nothing, go to Uni for 3 more years and do nothing, hell no!"

This back and forth went on for a while. I'd be lying....actually more exhausted if I was to put in the entire script of what was said. But we reached an agreement. She could see I wasn't backing down, I wasn't playing and I was dead serious about what I wanted to do.

She said, "You know I can't afford those courses."

"They can't be the only one doing them. I will look through and find some other places, but I'm not going back to college, that's for damn sure."

So she was going to back me, but she was going to be involved too because she would not allow me to just do nothing. But that was never my intention. I had a clear vision and there was nothing that was going to get in my way; this was going to work, period.

CHAPTER 4
– MARCHING THROUGH THE SNOW

The time must have been around November 2005. Now I had to practise what I was preaching. I had already seen, believed and knew this vision was for real and it would happen.

So I went right to work with the knowledge that I had about those courses; I had some keywords to play with. And I had found something, it was some kind of training organization which did those exact same courses. As a matter of fact, it may have been more extensive than what I had seen before. This was the first time I had seen certifications called MCP (Microsoft Certified Professional) which were individual certifications for each Microsoft exam you passed. Now this place did require some form of travelling as it was based somewhere in Tolworth.

So me and my mum headed down there to see what it was about. And one of the first things I learned was that anything which had a great layout, presentation, with amazing attention to detail, with a lot of catalogues...was going to cost an astronomical amount! And it was! But finding this out didn't happen until later on during my visit where I was given a competency-based exam to show if I was qualified.

In fact it was actually much higher in price and the course was even longer. At this moment I thought I'd failed because I knew if I told my mum this it would kind of prove her point on her wanting me to stay specifically in college and take the normal route. Eventually I did let her know this after we left and she understood why but she still had my back.

So I went back to the drawing board, doing some more research and then I came across a couple of websites that showed up as top results. The third one was another private institution which also focused on the same courses. What I liked were the testimonials and a structured breakdown over the fast track course which was specifically for adults Something clicked in it for me to go for this. A quick look through the website showed all of the same courses and more which I had seen before, so I knew I was on the right path. But what had really made me pay attention, was they had something called a Job Guarantee.

This was something special which they offered where if you had passed the exams for this course, if they didn't find you a job within a month they would not only give you the money back for the course but they would also give you the same amount back again, so that was...a lot! They also had a small caption next to it saying they had never paid it. So, it gave me all the confidence to believe in this.

Now I felt I had finally found what I was talking about all this time, and the perfect institute for doing this with, and with the motivation I had this could never fail. So as I had done with the other places I found, I had registered my interest on the web form.

Next day I had a call back from a representative there who had organized a meeting day/consultation down at their offices, which was situated just off Liverpool Street station.

Same team, me and my mum, went down there; we had just about made it there on time because we had got lost...well to be fair I got us lost; I thought I had the right way but ended up more down Threadneedle Street. At this time there wasn't a Google maps, or at least it wasn't as advanced where we had it on our phones back then so we had to either go with directions, A-Z, or just rely on our instinct.

After back and forth walking we finally reached there. Just looking around that office I had the feeling I knew my future was going to be solidified here. Instead of Mum getting involved like she would normally do she fell back this time, just waited in the reception area whilst I met not only the representative who had talked to me on the phone initially but also one of the owners.

After a brief talk, they did something which just made that motivation click into hyper mode. They let me sit in one of the classes for about 5 minutes to get an idea of how the classes were taught. At the time this was the A+ course which I heard so much about, which was really about the real technical details of PC hardware and also OS software. I had learned more in that 5 minutes than all the time I had spent in college! They had to tap me a couple of times in order to leave the preview of the course as I was hooked as soon as I got in there.

This was it! There was no going back or changing this one. I was donner (not a word but felt it) than done with college; that was over, it was all the way on this one. My mum at the time was using this MP4 player that I had bought a while back, she was watching the 50 Cent movie "Get Rich or Die tryin" at the time. That could have been reflective of how my mentality was when wanting to get on this course and really provide a successful visual to what my motivation had already written in essence.

All I know is that me and my mum went home with a different feel this time. A viewpoint that we had found the perfect place for me to continue my education, but my way, the right way and the only way for me.

The guys at Just IT were just as excited that I felt the way I did, I wanted in. The next part of this process was to attend a Job Guarantee interview which was similar to a job interview so I had to be fully suited for it. This was really important, because I desperately wanted that security of knowing once I beat those exams, and BELIEVE me they would have beaten how I was feeling I would get a job guaranteed, matched with their own statement saying they had never ever paid out after a month of not finding a job. Whether I had thought that was true or not, it didn't matter to me because whether they would guarantee I would get a job or not, I was guaranteeing myself a job.

(*Self-Motivation Point: Always believe in yourself enough to know you will accomplish what you came for regardless of whom or what will guarantee it for you. Your spirit can determine how driven you are and sometimes you have to also be mindful of where you want to be and not just leave it up to someone else to guarantee or solidify your future.*)

Now the suit requirement was resolved temporarily – I used one of my dad's old blazers. Might have been swimming a bit in it but it still worked for me and didn't look too bad to me anyway. Got my tie on, Vaseline on my shoes and it was time to do this.

So again the infamous me and mum team went back up there, me fully suited and booted. I didn't realise at the time I was going to be interviewed by someone else for it, even more the woman who actually interviewed me at the time I was like oh wow! But I grabbed my senses back after a few seconds because nailing the interview was more important than anything, no matter how good she looked to me at the time.

Interview-wise was more about my background, schools, colleges and I guess my determination for doing the course. My passion really did show throughout it, this was going to be mine with no one getting in the way of it.

After that was finished, the decision was then made: I was eligible to do the course; then we had to get down to business as to how much the course was going to be, which was an eye watering £5360.

This was primarily an adult-only course, so regardless of how young I was, this would have been no exception. But this time, there were actual flexible payment options available, well there was really one and this was something which had only been promoted at two banks, called a CDL (Career Development Loan). Only Barclays Bank and the Cooperative Bank took part in this, but Barclays had quickly shut down on this so Cooperative Bank were the only ones left doing it. The stipulations to the loan would be they would give me everything I wanted and then I had to pay it back every month for 5 years after 18 months from the initial grant of the loan. Now I was super confident, telling my mum over and over again "Trust me, there is no way I wouldn't get a role in 18 months, absolutely impossible".

We were all ready to go whilst speaking to the initial representative and also the owner, but then something happened where it could have all headed south very quickly...at least where my mum was concerned.

See, the great appeal about the Job Guarantee, was that it had guaranteed a job at a salary between £18k and £25k, which was literally a dream to be anywhere in that bracket. However...because I had literally just turned 18 I would really be a child doing an adult course and potentially the youngest person, period, to be doing an adult course such as this, so the risk factor for where their job guarantee was concerned was extremely high. Kind of like in blackjack the dealer having an Ace and the player has a hand of 15! So they proposed to drop the actual salary which would be guaranteed I would get on the job guarantee from £18k-£25k...to £12k-£16k. And it was safe to say my mum was not having or accepting that at all.

"That's not right, we can't be made to pay adult fees and have the salary chopped down that hard, that's not worth it."

Now...as greedy as an average young guy would be in this predicament, I thought about it and I didn't think this was such a bad idea. From my perspective I would have work experience, certifications, an actual stamp of some sort that would get me in the door, and also getting £12k-£16k a year was more than the nothing I was bringing in a year!

Though I told my mum this, she still wasn't really convinced about it, but I put it quite simply that it was really their guarantee not mine. That's not to say I wouldn't get a salary between £18k-£25k, which is exactly what they said as well.

She thought about it a little while longer, then eventually she agreed and signed the paperwork with me as I needed a parent to sign it as I was still too young. She wasn't entirely happy about doing it but she knew how much I wanted to do this and she had already agreed in her mind "well it doesn't mean you won't get what you want salary wise".

I had already known this, that's why I didn't pay it too much mind.

With the determination I had this was a done deal, now we had a bit of a countdown with the course date finalized, which was 13th February 2006. Time to hunt for the CDL loan. As the Cooperative Bank were the only one doing the loan, there was only one closest to us which was in Leadenhall Street.

This was the most gruesome process I had ever experienced when it came to any bank. The application form was approximately 10 pages back to back, and we needed an astronomical amount of proof of identity documentation. But not necessarily photo ID such as a passport etc it was more down to bank statements. At this time my bank had flat out refused to let me hold anything remotely like a debit card, so I had to rely solely on my book-based account which had to get printed each time I visited a branch.

I had to get photocopies of my book to be attached to the form which we sent alongside proof of authenticity of the original and photocopies and proof of postage. Two weeks later I had a response saying it had been rejected.

I rang them up and chased them for the reason why and they said it was because the photocopies couldn't be validated as to being real, so they advised I should go to my bank and get them specifically to photocopy it and for someone in the branch to officially stamp it.

Finally I got this printed in my bank and stamped as they suggested, and sent it again as a response to the rejection letter. Just before Christmas I received another rejection later saying the same thing.

This was starting to get annoying now, so when it turned to the new year I chased them up again. Now they said the person didn't date the photocopies and said that they needed to be validated as original and we don't allow the original to be sent to us.

So once again I went to the branch, got everything done like they said, rang the Co-op back and confirmed every single thing and they agreed this would be absolutely fine. Several weeks later they rejected it with the same thing again!

This time I lost it! I rang them up saying what the hell is this!? They tried to say the same thing but I said no! We're not doing this again, how can I get real original photocopies after you keep telling me this? So I asked would my actual bank book be proof?

They said absolutely it would. And I said, "Is it ok for me to send this?"

She said, "No sir this is not allowed!"

Yeah right, I didn't care and sent it to them anyway because I didn't have time for this almost 3 months of this, and it was literally time to start the course at this point with no funding at all organised! With this over my head I had to attend a pre meeting before the actual course at the private institute started, which was really a meet and greet of the other students who would be on the course. This was a great way for everyone to build up a rapport with each other beforehand. I wasn't nervous, but at the same time could feel the anticipation really building up at this point. Because I was about to make history as being the first eighteen year old to be doing an adult course. And that's a lot of pressure because you don't really have full knowledge on how good or bad that could be. You may be the first but will you be the first and succeed?

CHAPTER 5
– TIME TO MAKE HISTORY

1 3th February 2006; it was now time to start the course, first day. But at the time the course had not been paid for, and I was still waiting or expecting another useless answer from the Cooperative bank in regards to another rejection. Luckily me and my mum had already discussed it over the phone with the owner at the time who was still happy for us to start the course whilst we were trying to get an approval sorted, so this bought us some time. For that moment, I could relax and take in the first day, which was the beginning of history. No more college, not even University, this was like a whole different monster altogether, this was an out an out adult course, but it was met with the normality of my college days by bringing a packed lunch!

So here we are now the first day, Private classroom for approximately 15 of us in total for the duration of the 13-week course. The diversity of backgrounds really amazed me. Every kind of working and professional background you can imagine was there from diamond brokers, university leavers with degrees in IT, regular jobs, career changers. These guys had a lot more on the line than me in a real world circumstance, so I knew I had to really step it up here, but I was ready. First thing I clocked besides the diverse students, were the overwhelming amounts of McVitie's biscuits newly sealed, and Robinsons juices that were just waiting to be broken open and devoured, by me! Not like I had money to go to lunch so besides the sandwiches this was really the only other luxury I had.

We were now going through the introductions of each person so we could find out more about each person on the course. Then we had a little networking exercise/competition that consisted of seeing who remembered the most names of the people in the class, and we wrote down everything you remembered about their background. At this time the owner had stepped into the class just to observe and see how everything was going. He noticed I didn't really write anything in the notebook I had in regards to the competition – could have been I had nerves at the time they were doing this, but also because I have a tendency not to really write, my memory at times can hold an insane amount. I could almost look through it like diary pages. But I remember the owner taking a pen, writing down his full name and then putting down underneath it "He's a nice chap". Guess that was one name I was going to remember through the duration of this, and it was indeed!

The first module to kick off on this course was the A+ Hardware course, which was all about the history and complete technical breakdown of computer components. Strands of this were loosely covered by the teacher I remember in college who had mentioned one or two things close to this – he would have been the best teacher there at that point when I was in college, as far as I was concerned.

Break time came, and this may have been the most influential moment, as for the first day we were all taken to a pub/restaurant that was next door to the place where we were studying. We could order whatever we wanted, so knowing me at that time (and indeed nowadays) I went straight for a steak. One thing I remember was shooting a text to my mum like "They just took everyone out to eat for a steak meal". I was amazed by this because again I had only just gone from college where we were going to the local chicken shop that side, to having a steak meal, and in my mind all I could see was the cost compared to what I used to eat. My mum sent me a message back saying "that sounds great. And that's the life I want you to have always". That message may have solidified everything as of now!

After that experience... during the first week of the Just IT course, one of the members of staff had ask to speak to me for a short moment.

It was a quick word to let me know that my CDL loan had been approved and they had received the money and the whole course was now paid for.

For a moment I had forgotten about that loan because I was so frustrated with the process I had just sent every real physical copy of everything I had. But it was a relief to know that was completed, I really couldn't have dealt with another rejection letter for whatever reason they felt they could come up with as to why it was not approved.

In the meantime the course pushed on with several presentations mixed with practical knowledge that we could utilise on our PCs so that we could action out what we were learning, which was a great way to learn, and before we knew it, we were now coming to the end of the A+ Hardware course. We were told that we would have a one-week break so that we could study, for those who had plans to take the exam during this time. With all the time I had been desperate to get this opportunity? Oh I was for sure doing this exam. As soon as it was Saturday I studied, in fact I damn near imprisoned myself studying with the determination to read my study books from cover to cover. Everything from memorizing pages to testing myself and slaughtering the questions with a lot of extra detail added on to show how well-rounded was my understanding of what I was learning.

I studied so much that I lost weight, and studied so much to the point that my mum had to actually stop me. It's funny because the one thing I hear parents harp on about is "make sure you study" or "make sure you do your homework", but this determination was different because to me this wasn't just about some random coursework, this was my life and future! I naturally wanted to submerge myself in this study mode because they had to experience the five senses of my dedication. This was a time when I actually felt proud of myself for anything of this magnitude, and that it was an organic response to my self-motivation and not trying to pretend or put on a front for people. And I've never been motivated to be a reader of any sort, so it goes to show when you have that self-motivation with a keen interest, you will naturally gravitate towards the source of your success and if that involves reading then let's get it.

I had booked my exam for a Friday afternoon, so I went and put some added pressure on myself now studying and somewhat racing against the clock by testing myself, reading, testing myself and reading once again. I did have friends visit me once during this period, I guess to break away from the insane amount of studying I was doing. Even with them I was met with somewhat negative responses staring at the books I was studying saying "I can't do this, I don't know how you do this? This looks like a different language". Yes it is, the language of money! Well that's the motivation that guys our age could really relate to. It didn't stop me to keep pushing, and then it was Friday...D-Day.

Again no expectations but I was so anxious, nervous and hyped all at the same time. This was the day I could possibly establish myself within the food chain. I stuck to what was familiar to me in terms of areas where the test centre was located and that it could be the start of my career potentially being born in... Liverpool Street. It was booked at a small company based down Finsbury Circus. So here we go, enter in and go through the registration, I tell you all the checkpoints before you get into the exam room are so excruciating from filling out a long form, locking all of your belongings then reading an agreement form of terms and conditions. At this moment you can literally feel your heart ripping through your chest and the process of checking-in only prolongs this even more. Once I had signed everything and acknowledged to them I was ready, they took me into the exam room – you could hear a pin drop in there – and then they sat me at one of the computers and set up the exam and wished me good luck. Then the anticipation grew even bigger, this was it now, we have got to shine here. I developed a little strategy (at least it worked for me) which was to mark down on the card they gave me to write notes on, all the ones I know I got right and all the ones I wasn't entirely sure on. Then when I got to the end of all the questions, I went through all of them again and if I felt it was the correct answer I marked it alongside the right answers section, anything else I still was unsure of marked it wrong. Now the pass mark was only just over 50% so wasn't too high, but when it gets higher you better make sure you get them right! The structure of the exam itself was mainly multiple choice questions with some graphical interface questions for drag and drops. These exams, just like the process of the registration, of taking one where it prolongs the anticipation where at the beginning of them it asks if you would like to fill in a questionnaire about yourself and what areas you feel you are pro-efficient in. There used to be a myth that if you said you were strong in some areas it would alter the exam questions so we used to say we were weak in everything, but this didn't work after years of doing this.

My no-expectations mode took place, I must have gone through that exam in about 10 minutes! I was just on go from the moment I clicked start exam. Once I had gone through my quick little strategy I hit end exam. Again it prolonged the suspense by asking for another questionnaire again. Your heart damn near dancing now with the wait. Now one thing I wasn't aware of at the time was that it would tell you if you passed or not was going to be in the next few seconds. But what is worse being told straight away or being told after a few weeks or months? Can't have it both ways.

After the machine went to load what the result would be, it popped up and said…"Congratulations you have passed the exam. Your score is xxx out of 1000"! Followed by a printout of the results. The rush was so intense I didn't show a huge amount of excitement because it happened so damn fast. So I went to the reception and they just stared at me confused. They asked, "Did you just do the exam?"

I said, "Yeah."

They looked at each other confused again.

They asked, "Did you pass?"

And I said, "Yeah."

Now they were even more confused because it had literally been just over 10 minutes. They did say well done, congratulations after, but I think they were still stunned at the speed. That moment I felt my self-motivation was really predicting my future and that I had something here where I was right about everything I thought I could achieve.

This only made me more focused for the next round. So, after the week had finished we were back in the private institute for the A+ Software part of the course which was more focused on the role of an Operating System on a computer. I managed to catch-up with the rest of the class. It actually quite surprised me how many actually passed and the amount that failed on a first try. Not that I wanted in any way to hear that people failed it, but I guess for me it just validated that the exam I had done in 10 minutes was no walk in the park in any circumstance, because the last thing I wanted to feel was that it was something that came easy or anything was an easy road because I had taken a private course. You can go to a private course, university, anywhere, it makes no difference. If you don't put any kind of work in either one, failure will be imminent. And in this case the course was quicker than the normal route, but probably the same amount financially per university course term.

Soldiering through this course, here we go again, studying till I lost weight once again. Repeat the same process of going through the exam for A+ Software, this time it didn't take 10 minutes! Maybe because I knew this one I needed to beat to get the full certification (A+ Hardware & A+ Software formulate the A+ certification) and therefore I couldn't just do it with the same flare I had the last time. So I took my time; however, this time I was a lot more unsure of my answers and whether I had passed it or not, so I developed a way to slowly break the news to me where I used the notes card they give you to cover the entire screen once I clicked end exam.

I slowly pulled down the card just edging from the first word and all I remember it saying was "Congratulations...you...have...passed...your score was 789"! Literally it felt like my heart was beating insanely! I had now my very first IT industry certification at 18, from then on it was like I knew my future was set. I had started a trend where when I would come home to let my mum know if I had passed the exam or not, I'd either act like I didn't or talk about how hard it was...before I said I passed it!

A celebration, for it was due as everything I had put my foot down for when I demanded I was not going back to college had paid off. Oddly enough, I had received a phone call early the following week, Monday. It was from the administration staff from the college I was at previously.

They asked me, "Are you coming back to the course?"

I was laughing to myself at the time because I had forgotten, I didn't even mention anything, but after what I had just accomplished and thinking about the laughter I got for even wanting to attempt this idea, I quickly gained my composure and said "No, I'm not coming back" .

"OK, that's no problem, sorry to see you leave. If you could send back any course materials, pens, pencils or any other equipment back to us that would be great."

Yeah right, I was thinking, I never saw a full classroom for about a month, let alone course materials so I'm not sure as to where they thought I had stuff like that given to me because the rest of the students for damn sure didn't have any!

CHAPTER 6
– CHARGED UP

After some well-deserved and celebratory rest we now go back to the course, this time to start the Cisco CCNA (Cisco Certified Network Associate) course which was about networking with Cisco Hardware. Now this was the beast that had opened my eyes initially when the representative guy from the previous year showed me the salaries attached to these big certifications.

Though I was motivated to get into this, I realised this was a different beast because we were given 2 weeks' study break to go away and study for it.

I had started to somewhat establish myself amongst some of the guys in the course, as I was doing so much forward studying that when the teachers were asking questions and I was whispering or saying the answers to myself before the teacher did, and others looked at me looked at the teacher then looked at me.

Nobody had any intention of going for the CCNA exam, but I did! Over ambitious at this point but everyone was in my corner to pass it which was great morale. So here we go with the 2 weeks studying, the book was huge too but I kept the pace going. So much studying my mum had to tell me to take it easy and relax.

Here we go again with the exam now. This one was tough! I had come to learn during the course that I wasn't allowed to go back on questions – once I clicked next question that was it. I eventually folded on the toughness of the exam, I had already made it in my head knowing that I had failed. And once I clicked to end the exam, surprise surprise, I had failed. But it didn't matter too much, though I was upset at the time. The wild tenacity I had, got me to attempt it after 2 weeks' study and I knew it wasn't enough but I was hungry to get on. The score I had achieved wasn't far away from passing, considering the pass mark was a very high 85%.

I returned back to the course, this time for the Linux+ exam which was similar to the A+ software exam but instead of Windows this was a Linux/Unix focus. Perhaps an early opener for me to get more used to command line and developing, which helped me to pick up more the scripting languages available today. Again, I wanted revenge from the CCNA exam so I pushed hard with this one.

Would you believe that I had actually failed the exam by one point? One point! You couldn't make it up. To me I had passed! It's tough to bounce back from failing an exam but it psychologically makes it worse knowing you failed by a point. I remember earlier on the course another student had failed an exam and wasn't feeling great about it and the owner of the private institute said "Just because you failed the exam, doesn't mean you don't know anything about the subject matter or that you are not a specialist or if you are, it just means you didn't pass the exam". To me this meant a lot to hear because it helped me deal with any exam which I did feel I'd passed, as well as influencing me to study above and beyond the initial exam requirements.

*(**Self-Motivation Point:** Do not let a "loss" or a "failure" determine your future. You have to sometimes handle loss or failure in order to learn and bounce back. It's all about being motivated to persevere with your goal.)*

CHAPTER 7
– SHAPING AND MOULDING

The next two days back on the course we had two important exercises which were even more crucial than just trying to ace all exams; it was called something like a job searching day. It entailed all of us coming fully suited and booted to emulate a real work day. Everything from searching for a job to a mock interview. This day did so much for me you couldn't even put it into words because the job searching part I may have absorbed more than anybody on that day; the reason I say that is because that was when I first saw the job site called "JobServe", which to date every role I've ever had I got through it (though LinkedIn is now starting to take over).

Learning how to structure our CV was a great exercise displaying our personal profile and the courses and exams we had completed which gave us (especially me) a voice that I never had before which could command a response from an agency to have interest in me. But I took mine to a different level...because even though we were just doing an exercise to see who could find out who the end client was, with as much information about the role and organisation as we could, somehow the conversations I had with them turned into a real "Yes send me your CV and we will get you an interview".

So my mock CV ended up looking so appealing to them it started circulating through agencies and from that day and every day for several years I was getting calls for jobs. It had started a frenzy. I was addicted to this feeling, because the perspective was that being in demand was the most important and the 500 degree temperature of the battery in my phone reflected that.

After that we started mock interviews, to see how our responses to technical questions and competency-based questions would turn out. I don't really remember every question asked but I remember there was a key question which everyone thought I had aced, maybe it looked more impressive because I was only 18 at the time. The mock interview had 3 interviewers...probably the average these days for interview processes.

The next day was an exercise in which everybody was to perform a presentation to the whole class. I was extremely nervous to do this and I had it my mind it wasn't going to go well. I already had a subject matter which was all about muscles in the body because at the time I was really heavily into weight lifting so the motivation on the subject matter was there, I had everything prepared. On the day, I was meant to go on early which was perfect for me because I had the energy to do it, but because they ended up changing some of the schedules and some guys overran it drained the energy from me to the point where all I felt was pure nerves. Then it was my turn now.

Mine was about 10-15 minutes, all about different muscle groups and I took questions from the class. To be honest I was glad when it was finally over. I hated the feeling of doing it. Some guys in the class said that the presentation was quite alright, they could see I was nervous but they felt I'd done good. Didn't feel like it to me but it was somewhat comforting.

But then, later that day we had a meeting individually with a coordinator at the private institute who was grading the presentations. They called me in and basically said "I didn't think the presentation was good at all and I gave it 3/10. Normally I would make you do it again but I'll let you off this time".

I'm not sure what the purpose was to tell me in this way, but I wasn't really too fussed about it because the grade they gave me reflected how I felt giving it, so maybe it just confirmed how I felt it went. I told some of the guys the grade I got and they got quite angry.

"3!?, no that's ridiculous I mean I would have said a 6 at least, but 3!?" To be honest I was shocked that they were shocked! I personally didn't feel it went that bad when I reviewed the presentation itself, but I can't really tell how my performance shows to someone else when they are visibly nervous.

About half way home, I had a couple of email messages from the same coordinator at the private institute. They were apologising over and over again about the harshness and the harsh grade they gave me. I was quite surprised, I'm not sure exactly where it came from. I think some of my colleagues may have complained about the grade that I had received. The coordinator also went on to say that they didn't think my presentation was that bad at all in all honesty and that they were sorry I was so unhappy with my mark.

I said it was absolutely fine and I wasn't unhappy with it. I may have been being a bit nice, but whether it was the right or wrong grade it was something I had to build on regardless. Because if I don't treat this as a learning curve, I won't improve and to go around thinking every bad rating I get is just a mistake was not the way I wanted to proceed, so I took it in a positive way.

(*Self-Motivation Point: Always take feedback on board whether it's good, bad, biased or un-biased. Nobody wants to hear that they are doing bad or terrible, or about areas marked for improvement, but you don't evolve without it. Being ignorant towards feedback will not serve you in the long run.*)

After a one week break, we went to do the last modules called MCPs (Microsoft Certified Professional) for the Windows Sever 2003 and Windows XP operating systems at the time. The private institute had a new office location which they moved to, close to Petticoat Lane. We were waiting outside for a few minutes for the doors to open then one of the students came over to me and was saying, "I overheard a conversation with some managers or directors, they were all talking about you and how much of a genius you are."

"Really?" I said. I didn't understand why at the time, maybe it was because I was the only one insane enough to attempt every exam after the study breaks we had – either way it gave me a good morale boost I guess.

So we continued the last two weeks doing the MCP course back to back... after that the 13 week course had been completed. It was a great achievement for me the fact I was able to hang with and keep up with adults in a strictly adult-only course. So we had a ceremony where everyone was given a certificate of completion attached with a speech specific to each person so you could guess as to which person they were referring to before they got their certificate.

Now the next phase, which was for each person to be sorted with a work placement which would normally be between 6-8 weeks of a work experience based role. At the time my phone was still ringing quite frequently for real jobs, but this work placement would be a great thing to experience. At the same time this was where I started to feel the real resistance of being so young and competing against adults when it came to the same position for work placement.

I had about 4 work placement interviews I had attended all over London, and each of them had passed over me and the feedback was simply because they decided to go with someone who was older. At this point it started to slightly frustrate me, because I really did put an effort in on every interview and to just get looked over because of my age started to take a bit of a toll on me. But as the saying goes "good things come to those"...well at least they say that how I was thinking. But you can never see this coming, only can relate to the frustration happening as of right now.

After a couple of interview mock exercises at the private institute, they gave me some good tips which I was able to put to use regarding talking about my key skills, which became an ability I was able to manipulate to be able to control the interview a bit more.

Then, another interview request for a work placement came out of the woodwork and this was at a recruitment organization that specialised in the legal sector and they were based down Old Broad Street next to Liverpool Street, so quite familiar surroundings after doing the course across the street.

At that point of getting prepared for the interview and attending on the day, I guess I still had an ounce of the frustration I had experienced already from being slighted because of my age and I could feel it was still there. This is a great motivation at times as it gives almost a "nothing to lose-ish" mentality so you end up having a more adaptive mindset. And I'm glad to say it did pay off in this interview. It was a good conversation with the IT Manager at the legal organisation about my ambitions, hobbies as well as what my strengths were. I left the interview feeling like I did alright...then again I had felt like this before so I already had a pre-conceived notion that I knew how this was going to turn out.

I then had a call from the private institute in regards to feedback to the interview and I was told that the legal organization wanted me to attend a second interview which was great news! Finally I had got an opportunity to gain some experience now. In addition to this feedback he had some other comments which were about my nails having dirt in them and also dirt in my collar. My first initial thought was "Wow! People really pay attention to small details like that!?" More the dirt in my nails I was more taken aback by rather than the collar as I may have been using a shirt I had used on a previous interview so that was more understandable. But not only did I get feedback which was good news overall, but the additional points gave me a lesson that those comments would never need to be said again! And they always stuck with me because it might seem like a small thing but if you keep letting the small things slide it'll be a failure (points to whoever knows where that line originates from).

*(**Self-Motivation Point:** Presentation is everything, especially when it comes to how you look. Keeping yourself smart and looking the part as you are the brand, and when you are presented well then you represent your brand well.)*

Here we go with the second interview, this one was an even more relaxed type of conversation. The question and answer that solidified it for me was when the IT Manager asked me, "What football team do you support?"

My answer was, "Well in terms of football clubs I support Man Utd, international team-wise I support Brazil. But then again even though I may have supported those teams, at the end of the day I really support good football regardless of the teams." It may have been a slick way to avoid being called a glory hunter as well, but he really did like that answer.

Next day I heard back confirming that I had been awarded the work placement, which couldn't be better news at the time. I felt vindicated more than anything.

CHAPTER 8
– CLIMBING THE CAREER LADDER

First day I started I was nervous. No idea of what to expect. I was then introduced to another guy who was also there on a work placement who had been there about 4 weeks already and had about 2 weeks left to go. He really showed me the ropes in terms of the duties we had, which entailed setting up new desk phones, setting up new computers and going through the helpdesk system which they had where other workers would submit issues or requests through. I soaked up everything as much as I could, just observing everything in my very first simulated job position. I really had to take in the real working atmosphere, was a trip. Just visualizing where I am thinking to myself of how far I came from the decision to leave college and now getting a real feel of what it can and would be like. A career was at stake for me and I intended to grab it with both hands.

When it came to the lunch breaks they were inspiring to me. I remember looking around at everybody fully suited and booted, briefcases, getting lunch, thinking one day this will be me doing this. Walking around Liverpool Street station watching a sea of people queuing up at McDonald's, having obnoxiously loud business conversations on their phones. The whole visual was just doing it for me. Course I did snap back into reality especially back then when I was still having packed lunches with sandwiches to get me through the day and I can't stand sandwiches for lunch, cannot eat anything cold for lunch.

As the day went by I had a phone call about a job which sounded quite interesting. I'd only been on a work placement for one day and I was already being headhunted. I couldn't believe it. And from that day on, even more it just kept coming. Throughout my time at the work placement I was just getting calls non-stop, which eventually turned into interviews non-stop. So many agencies were ringing me on the helpdesk phone that connected to my desk where I was working. It's strange because the guy whom I worked with on his final 2 weeks on his work placement didn't receive any. But then he did get a call when I was there, so literally one call? Made me wonder what exactly was special about me?

Now we get into the interviews. I had flooded the JobServe Job board with my CV. I had constantly updated my CV with experience I had gained alongside the exams and courses I had done, and eventually I managed to score my first interview. It was for a 1st line support engineer at an online gaming company and was paying about £18k at the time. Bear in mind I still had the job guarantee contract which was fixed between £12k-£16k. But I always knew that I had it in me to surpass this bracket, and so did the Owner at the Private Institute. Not my smartest move but I took my mum along with me; then again maybe that's harsh because I had assumed it would have been an office that would have had a reception area, but we ended up opening the door to the whole office that looked like a trading floor. I explained to one of the staff that I had an interview and we waited in the corner of some kind of office; eventually the interviewer came out greeted me...and also my mum. This is where I felt strange about it because now we are both here when it's really just me being interviewed, but nonetheless we did the interview, just me and the interviewer. We ran through a few competency based questions but the interview wasn't exactly long. I had experience in interviews already from chasing down work placements so I kind of knew the process, but I'm pretty sure that the interviewer "knowing" my mum was waiting for me and even him addressing her as "Mum"....I'd say that was pretty much a wrap from there. I wasn't concerned about feedback for that role.

(Self-Motivation Point: Please don't bring your parents to an interview with you!)

It didn't matter, it was all good; at least I got some experience in the field of a paying job role so I went back to grinding looking for a role whilst doing my work placement.

During the time I spent between finishing the private course and working at my current work placement and trying to find a job, I used to have an old Nokia phone which I would preload with music and eventually ended up forming my own playlist. I had a name for it which would be called the "Soundtrack of Success".

I would listen to it on a daily basis, the exact same songs in the exact same order. It put me in a mind to focus on my future and the goals at hand and it did a lot for me.

Here is the exact list of the tracks I had on this playlist to give an idea:

1. Big Noyd – Shoot Em Up Part 1
2. Rick James – Give It To Me
3. Mobb Deep – G.O.D Part III
4. Cyssero – Crack Music
5. Big Noyd – Shoot Em Up Part 2
6. Pharrell – Mamacita
7. Papoose – Hustle Hard
8. Jim Jones – Harlem
9. Pharrell & Kanye West – Number One
10. 50 Cent – Pimp Pt 2
11. NORE – I'm a G.

I had set up various interviews and I never really took a step back and looked at the sight of an 18 year old, fully suited and booted and looking for an IT position. I remember I met up with a director of a small agency to talk about roles and what was available in the market (I still have her business card to this day).

And she asked me "how old are you?"

"18," I said.

She said, "That is fantastic, I've never seen this before in my life, someone so young with the way you are presenting yourself and looking for a job? It's amazing!" I never looked at it like that, but I guess it is a sight to see. When I look at the average 18 year old nowadays I really still see the child growing into an adult, so now I can kind of appreciate more how it came across...especially with the amount of interviews I was doing, and not to mention I had an extremely young looking face then so I probably looked even younger to them! But sometimes where your tenacity is concerned, to get on the career ladder can put you in a position you don't really want to be in just for the sake of having a job. For example, I had interviewed for a role which required someone to work a graveyard shift for IT support and it went brilliantly and the interviewer was wanting to offer me the job and said I'm going to bring in my boss to have a chat with you as an informal chat. We had a chat and I felt overall it had to be a done deal. Only to be let down with a phone call the next day or so saying I didn't get the job.

"What!? How? Why?"

The feedback was that I was too young. Again that frustration came flooding back...but to rationalise it I think they were right. Did I really want to commit to doing a graveyard shift role? Sometimes even though you may want something badly enough doesn't always mean you should fully compromise your comfortable requirements and to have a role you could eventually hate would not help you in the long run. My naivety could have been my downfall at times.

I progressed with several interviews all over London, sometimes 2-3 in the same day. Feedback was a general consensus of "you were so close but someone just had that bit more experience". Whilst it's not bad feedback it's a tease at the same time. Especially when I heard they "would love to take you on later" and my naivety again led me to believe this was true – but it never was.

One interview I'll never forget, which was where I experienced a point of doubt before you hit the nothing-to-lose feeling. I had an interview for a helpdesk role for a position at a marketing organisation which was based in Putney. Putney would have been a bit of a journey to commit to when I was living at Elephant and Castle and I would refuse to use an underground train (can't stand them)...but my eagerness to get a job just looked right past it.

I felt I did very well on that interview, I had sharpened my technical skills sword so was ready for any technical questions thrown at me. I had questions prepared for the interviewers, researched the company background etc. and I felt quite good about myself. A few days later I got a call from the agency representing me and they said..."Unfortunately you didn't get the role. But you were so close they took on another guy but they liked both of you and wanted to create another position for you." Again...with the naivety I had believed that...thinking that in some kind of way this was like an offer. So I stayed on that feedback chasing up every week for about month thinking this was a promise they would keep...sadly this was not the case. I knew I was close to nailing this but it just seemed like I was so far away at the same time. My mum said to me, "You will get your time. You've heard that you were second and so close so many times, eventually you will be first." That's what I needed to hear just to really keep me in the game.

Back to the drawing board looking for roles, whilst I was at my work placement getting the occasional McDonald's fries with my sandwiches which I was reluctant to eat. A new guy had started at Career Legal, and it was my turn to show somebody the ropes, which was a good way of showcasing my responsibility...felt managerial-ish for a moment. My phone was still ringing non-stop, till eventually I had another interview request; this one was from a fashion giant that were based next to Paddington Station.

I had decided to take my mum with me once again. Why? I couldn't tell you, but guess I felt I needed some kind of moral support after the countless feedbacks of being looked over. But I did make sure there was a reception area beforehand for her to just wait in a café somewhere. Luckily for confirmation, this time there was a reception area where she could sit in till I eventually got called away for the interview, and they had no clue my mum was there, so that was perfect. I had gone into my "nothing to lose" persona and didn't hold back in going for the opportunity at hand. I had so much feedback saying I was second I was looser with my approach which enabled me to be more adaptive to the interviewers. Competency based questions around how I would handle multiple tasks came up and I responded with how I would prioritise the tasks at hand which they seemed to resonate with quite well. I felt I did well but hey I thought that last time so I wasn't going to hold my breath. I do remember I was wearing a long black mac and everyone in Paddington Station thought I worked in the station and kept asking me for directions. As I knew the underground quite well I didn't catch on, until almost everybody kept coming up to me and I just said, "I don't work here!" They laughed at me but I wasn't really in a joking mood.

Days went by and I worked through my work placement where the IT Manager entrusted me with more responsibility to prove myself. Eventually I built up a rapport with the staff there who were saying great things about the abilities I displayed, so this gave me some confidence that I needed and it felt good to be recognized in that way. That same day I had got a call back from the interview I had. It was a direct call from the client as the role was advertised directly with them. I was thinking to myself let's just get this over with, you tell me I came second so I can just push on and get on with my placement. But to my disbelief they invited me to a second stage interview! I really didn't know what to think? It wasn't a celebratory moment because I just felt I may have got further but it was just a longer process to be told 'no'. But it was still something, so I got myself prepared for whatever I may face again, no expectations.

Regardless of how up or down I felt I still remained optimistic. I used to have a text document with a list of everything I would buy when I got my first job. Everything you can imagine the average 18 year old would list:

- HDTV (they were pretty new at this time)
- Xbox 360
- Trainers
- Clothes

No expenses were spared in my dreams there with that list! It was actually a lot longer than this but it gives you a good idea.

But anyways, I made my way back down to attend the second interview. By myself this time! I went to meet the IT Manager there thinking technical grilling part two. But it was so totally opposite to what I thought it was going to be. He basically said this wasn't an interview, it was just to come and meet the team. And they knew I was the right person for the job after the interview I had. I didn't know what to think! I went around shaking hands, being introduced to other managers and vice versa. Talking about the certifications I had (we will come back to this part later as I had developed a strategy which would eventually end up backfiring), so after that we walked around the building and the IT manager telling me what my salary was going to be saying "See you're going to be getting 18k at 18!" If I could do anything celebratory in my mind I did so. If your brain could do back flips then mine sure was. I remember having some kind of whatever when I was in the toilet washing my hands, still soaking wet didn't dry them probably down to the excitement of everything. After we wrapped up everything I shook the IT Manager's hands and he obviously now had soaking wet hands also!

I remember leaving and ringing my mum's phone but it was off the hook! At the time she was a cashier at a supermarket so answering the phone at this time was not allowed at all. I remember just ringing and ringing and I got so annoyed I left a voicemail saying "I had something important to tell you but you missed it now so going back to work".

Whilst I was waiting for the bus I had a ring back while she was in the toilet saying "I can't really talk but what is it?"

I kept saying, "I got the job I got the job, Rocco Rocco!"

Now to explain the Rocco part of it, that was kind of the key word or secret word for when we had good news of getting the job. It really came from the joke Eddie Murphy had on the comedy special "Raw". So my mum was happy but she really couldn't express it over the phone so she had to end the call shortly after, but I understood completely.

So I made my way back to my work placement after an excruciating bus journey back as I just didn't want to take the underground train back. I saw the IT Manager just to have a quick catch up with him and head back to my duties and he asked, "Hi Dujon how did it go?"

I waited for a few good seconds whilst he had his head down and I said, "I got the job!"

He looked up at me immediately, also in shock because it's not always common to be told you have the job at an interview in this case. He congratulated me on everything, but here was the bad part for him. They wanted me to start next Monday so obviously I had to wrap up the work placement. But he understood and was very encouraging of it, so it was all good.

I remember later on that day when I was working I had a phone call. It was one of the recruitment agents at the private institute where I'd completed the course. They asked, "Did you get a job offer?"

"Yes," I replied.

"That's amazing. What salary did they offer?"

"£18k," I replied.

They were ecstatic, but especially me, because I knew just like my mum knew and also just like the Owner at the private institute had confidence in me, that I would have got what I wanted and that was the biggest achievement for me. I had proved it to myself. Even the staff at my work placement were sad I was going saying "He can't go, he's a genius". I would not have imagined that I of all people would have the word genius keep following me around.

So my list of all the things I wanted to purchase would surely come true, that's for sure; the first victim would eventually be my mum's MBNA credit card as no one would give me a damn debit card myself...but that's another story to moan about.

My last days at Career Legal were really manning the phone and helpdesk queues with the other guy at his work placement. Our main conversations used to really be fantasizing about salaries and we were constantly trying to guess what the IT Manager's salary was. That there was motivation to push even further.

On the last day I was given a grand gesture with a chocolate cake they had made for me to celebrate my new job, with also a promise I would get some of the staff a discount on clothes. I learned a lot there and established a lot. My phone remained ringing off the hook, I had real experience laid out on my CV and now had a new job and a salary to go with it. This was now the birth of my career.

I caught up with a couple of the guys I went to college with. One of them didn't believe me at all so I had sent him a screenshot of the contract with the relevant parts to me blacked out. They couldn't believe it! Everything I had said back then I had made into reality. I was told that after hearing how I had done, a lot of those students dropped out of the BTEC course immediately after. There's no "I told you so" type of message to this, it's all about standing your ground with what you want to achieve and hopefully they were able to be influenced by what I done and do the same or even better than me.

CHAPTER 9
– BEGINNING OF MY CAREER

Here we go. The first day at my new job. And real job! I started sometime in June 2006 which was almost a month after I had completed the adult-only course.

I don't remember a damn thing about this day! Well I remember having the induction, of course, and meeting the rest of the helpdesk team that I would be working with. I had a mixture of eagerness and nerves as this was so much bigger than the organizations I had either worked for or done my work placement in, so I felt like I had to pick things up quickly to keep up. At the time I still didn't really have any money so I was still fortunate enough to get pocket money from my dad at that time of £15 a week. At the time I started I was in the middle of the month so I wouldn't get paid until the end of July, which did take a toll on me. One of the finance managers asked me if I would be ok with waiting till then or they could perform a payment run at the end of June just so I could get some kind of remuneration but I said it's ok I'll wait till end of July. Guess I was happy that I had something so waiting a little longer to get paid wasn't a huge deal to me.

I remember I was using the toilet one day and there was this cleaning lady who I would regularly talk to during my time here. She knew I was a new employee and was asking me what I was working as and how much I was getting. She was like "18k? Nobody at 18 gets 18k!" She was ecstatic for me. I really liked her, and when she said this it always made me feel accomplished for what I had achieved, even to this day.

In my new role, I had similar duties to those at my work placement in regards to going through the helpdesk queues, but I also started to get my first taste in building machines using tools such as Norton Ghost which consisted of using a CD to boot up and build the desktop PCs and laptops in the build room they had. Locating staff in that building was not easy at all as the amount of floors and number of staff was huge! I did start to build up relationships between some of the staff as I regularly had to go to them to fix issues during my floor walks and managing of helpdesk tickets.

I had my fair share of challenges and incomplete tasks that I had, was a lot more in my shell in those days. So sometimes asking for help or assistance wasn't really second nature for me back then. I remember one time when I was in the build room trying to build a computer using the Norton Ghost and one of the buttons on the physical machine had fallen inside the machine. So I had to open up the machine to retrieve it and of course tried to fit the power button back on. So, my innovative idea was to stick it back on from the inside using sellotape. Now at the time I thought this was a great idea! Well it was my idea of initiative anyway. Until the IT Manager came in just to check how I was getting on and noticed it and I let him know the power button had fallen out but had a way to fix it. But then he was able to just fit the button back on with a bit of force...so my initiative pretty much went right out the window. As it was my first real actual job I was bound to make a few mistakes here and there, but I guess my closed up personality at the time may have not taken on a thought process to open up a bit more.

Unfortunately some bad news came. The cleaning lady I had befriended on my first day and who I spoke to quite regularly, had passed away. I was in shock as was everybody else. I actually wanted to attend the funeral, but at that time I didn't have any money still, but I would always remember her as giving me my very first feeling of actually being proud of myself.

During this time I was still working through the position and was feeling the anticipation of getting my first pay slip, as I had opted to wait until the end of July to get paid so when it came to social events that normally involved going out to eat, I had to pass. I didn't want to be the third wheel, third broken wheel at that. I made up an excuse here and there that sounded plausible to get out of them as I didn't want to actually really let it be known I was feeling the effects of not having any money back then. But then it got to the end of the month and they used to leave the pay slips on everyone's desk. And finally I got to open it and...wow! Not only just my first pay cheque but it was the biggest I had ever seen my name on...ever! I don't know how much my parents get paid but all I knew was that this was mine with my name on it! The IT Manager at that time was excited for me too because he knew how long I had waited so he figured that some serious spending would happen. Not quite serious but that MBNA credit card did get stress tested. In fact if you are able to find my Myspace profile, that picture was me back in those times and everything you saw there was pretty much bought with that first pay.

I remember I showed my mum that pay slip and she was in shock. Obviously it was slightly more inflated with the extra two weeks or more on top. My dad had visited one time and he looked at the pay slip. And his face changed in a strange way. He said with a slightly confused face, "This is slightly more than me." That made my excitement thrive even more but of course I didn't really want to show it because it kind of felt like he felt uncomfortable about it. Of course no pocket money was going to happen again at this point now I was getting paid!

My mum allowed me to keep the entire first pay which was brilliant for me. All I know was I was performing David Blaine tricks with that pay slip. The most extravagant purchase I made was this watch – Rose Gold (real rose gold) and real diamond (about 0.5ct though) all over the face and inside the face. It was an Aqua Master watch and the watch looked insane – I spent over £500+ on it. The Myspace profile picture does show a glimpse of it if you are able to find it.

CHAPTER 10
– BUMPS IN THE ROAD

Whilst the good times may have been rolling on that front, more challenges came about where my role was concerned.

There was a time when I had to lock the build room before finishing work which was a mandatory process to stop any staff from entering and possibly stealing equipment. So I had gone ahead and locked the build room door with the key allocated for it. Next to the room was a little locker which contained all of the keys and that's where I placed the key back in and then locked the locker with the actual master key. I double checked the build room door was locked and that was me done for the day. But when I came in the next morning there seemed to be a slight bit of chaos happening. The IT Manager asked me if I had the key for the locker which contained the keys, which I did and gave to him, as I believe this was like a shift rotation and the person who had the key that came in essentially was able to open the build room. But somehow...not only was the key inside the locker for the build room missing, but the actual build room door room was opened. I was confused because I am pretty sure I had checked this. And because the IT Manager at the time had somewhat been given a talking to from his boss, I knew this was going to be a problem for me. So the IT Manager called a meeting inside that very build room explaining the seriousness of what had just happened and explaining how this key (the one to open the build room) was missing. I can't remember where he said he found it but it wasn't in the locker. So after we were able to leave from the catch-up, the IT Manager called me back over to talk to me privately. I knew this was not going to be good.

"I specifically told you to make sure this door was locked and I came in in the morning and it was wide open! Anybody could have come in and took everything in here!"

I was trying to think fast because I was so confident there was no way that door was unlocked or open, but because of the panicking in that situation I had really second guessed myself and I no longer remembered if I definitely did lock it or not. So with me really folding under pressure I accepted the responsibility for it. I remember saying "I know I was supposed to...but I didn't". Paraphrasing here, but I was really apologetic about this. Regardless of whether I did or didn't, I was the only one with the key for the locker and had been given the responsibility to do it, so had to accept the blame for it. Of course another issue which came up was that I had been storing laptops in my drawer which were laptops that had been freshly built to allocate to new starters of the company. But the main issue was that my drawer wasn't locked and anybody could have taken them. I remember the IT Manager had asked me to check my drawer when I already knew he had removed them beforehand because he may have checked my drawers to see if I had the key there. Of course I checked and saw the laptops had gone – he eventually stated that he had taken them and put them back in the build room as well. He had then got his boss to talk to me for a minute to say something to the effect of "I don't want to have given you a warning over this, but be more careful next time". I didn't know what was going to happen but I knew I was going to have to make sure I kept my head down and start to really work a lot better and to keep closer track of what I was doing.

I had about a month left on my probation period so I spent this time really working as hard as I could. I started to build up a relationship with a certain department as I was closing a lot of helpdesk calls, the majority of them being good feedback not being re-opened, though I did have the odd incomplete job here and there and some technical issues can be like that depending on the scenario. But I was doing so well with certain departments that in fact so much to the point that they were calling me directly to help them and not even logging the call to the helpdesk or asking anybody else to help them for that matter. Though this was great for me, at the same time it could have been worse for me because it meant there was no track of what I was doing when I was away from my desk for long periods of time.

So my probation period meeting day came. I honestly had no clue what this was, but came to realize this was a mandatory clause in any job position to assess how an employee was doing after 3 months. I knew I had made some mistakes and hiccups along the way, but I felt overall I had done alright. Not to the best of my standards, but still.

The IT Manager had rounded it off to say basically that I was very inexperienced. Which to be fair I could see that. But then certain points made in the meeting I thought were just mind boggling. For example, I had built up a relationship with quite a lot of the staff whom I had solved regular issues for, a couple may had not been 100% complete for whatever reason but I had good relationships with them. I said this in the meeting and the IT Manager responded saying "well I spoke to some of them as well for feedback...and some of them said that it was...difficult to know....what you were going to do...then also" kind of just made the point and then trailed into another point altogether which I didn't get because to me that could not have been true. Not with the countless thank you and such and such I was getting so I don't know who or where that feedback came from. Now the strangest part of the feedback was when he said that I slouch in my chair. Slouching? That was actually a critique for a probationary period meeting? When we were allowed to come in our own clothes and all our chairs all leant back? And not to mention there were guys who had their legs stretched out and on the desk with shoes off! He did mention that and said he would talk to them about that as well, but it never looked like that happened as they were still doing it even after that. Then another point was made that I had my headphones around my neck (I still do this btw) and felt it wasn't very professional. And also he brought up the time when I tried to use the sellotape on the power button and that it's not the way we do things here. So overall he said he wasn't really happy with the performance so he wanted to extend the probationary period by another month. He explained that he didn't want to see me go and no one else did because "you are trying and have potential", and even went on to say he was looking at eventually giving me a pay rise, so there was an incentive to step my game up at least to prove it worthy to them, but in the back of my mind I wasn't sure if there was anything more I could have done because it just seemed like their mind was made up on me...but I wasn't going to give up.

But the last part about it was that he wanted to see my certificates, which to me was the biggest alarm bell, and I'll explain. See at the time I had only completed the A+ Certification and of course the courses and the attempts on all the other exams. But because on the second interview, which was really a meet and greet to welcome me in, I had said I had those certifications because I was so eager to impress and clench the deal. And my perspective was that I had set a strategy to set goals for myself where I would have them stated on my profile for what I hadn't done yet but then fulfil them immediately after, but of course you can't really do that because it doesn't really compute to others the same way. So now I really was in a panic here. One of the things I did do was attempt the MCP exam for Windows XP which I did study hard for and sat the exam a few days later. During the test, there was actually some kind of mistake going on where it would repeat the same question 4 times – I knew the answer but it seemed like something went wrong. Then it eventually said I had failed the exam but the pass mark didn't make sense. So I had complained and put a request in, but I really felt the clock ticking in my role here.

The IT Manager wanted to check I was ok after the meeting and I said "I know what to do now and where I need to pick up and it was more like a motivational speech" and he seemed to love that response and thought process.

So the next two weeks I really did put in a great effort, and even opened up more and asked for help when needed. But the certificates question came up again and was starting to make me frustrated because it was more than once he asked me. So I brought in my A+ one but he didn't see the rest, so I think this prompted him to do an investigation on me and he had contacted someone at the private institute I did the course in. Not sure who but he had found the exams I took, certifications and courses I did.

I was off sick one day, and then came back in the next day and the IT Manager had asked to speak to me alongside the internal recruiter who had sent me the job offer. He said he had spoken to someone where I completed my course and found out what I had done, and was starting to interrogate me about the certificates. But I had explained the courses I had done and the exams I did, the ones I passed and didn't pass. I don't really remember what happened after but I remember it was lunch time and he had said that I could take all the time I needed. I guess it was meant to be breathing space to get my story or thoughts together. I remember calling my mum in an absolute panic because I knew they were going to use this to possibly fire me. I just didn't understand the massive emphasis at the time. The certifications didn't have anything to do with what my role entailed, and I didn't think my performance was bad enough to start an interrogation. But the fact of the matter is I had said this so now I had to face it from a mistake which I made.

After lunch, they had asked to talk to me again in the build room. I had said that "I wanted to still stay but if it looks like I lied then I guess...".

But the IT Manager said "it doesn't look like you lied, you have lied" and went on to say that the rest of the IT Helpdesk staff were basically carrying me and that the work I did wasn't that good and that I also tried to bullshit his boss when the build room incident happened. So I was given an ultimatum where either I could resign and leave, or I could stay to basically eventually get fired. So I chose to resign, and the IT Manager had said I could leave early. I had shaken their hands and then eventually signed out and left. It was easily the most embarrassing experience I had to go through at that time. I remember taking a peak around the corner into the build room just before I left, and saw them laughing and joking with each other. Almost as if nothing had happened.

But I learned a lot from this experience. Regardless of how I viewed my performance or not, whether I felt the feedback was warranted, not warranted or whether I may have felt I was penalised for lying or making mistakes, it means nothing. At the end of the day it doesn't change the situation and you have to accept it. It's the only way you can move forward and learn from your mistakes. If I went around thinking at that time 'I was done wrong I was done wrong', I wouldn't be anywhere where I am today. I lied to try to impress where I probably didn't need to and I paid the price for it. I had rung my mum to let her know exactly what had happened and she was very sad about it but I said, "Don't worry. Because this is not going to be the end of anything. I will get another role and we will look back on this". And I meant every word, because I had accepted and understood the situation and this allowed me to build and move forward and this situation would NEVER! Happen again.

CHAPTER 11
– WEATHERING THE STORM

I did have a lot of added responsibility and pressure because at the time I told my mum she could change her job role from full time to half time now that I was working because I knew she hated that job and had so many issues there and working extremely unsociable hours. But I was more than determined to make sure I would be back in the game and I wasn't going to let either of us down. The amount of headache it took to get here was enough, so now I had more of a stamp and an established job history, it could only work in my favour.

I had to go back to the office where I resigned from a day or so later as I had to officially hand in my letter of resignation. So I met up with the internal recruiter and he asked if I wanted to go down to see the IT Manager. I always thought that was a weird question. After the embarrassment I experienced you would want me to walk through everybody and talk to him? No, it was better he just met us in the meeting room. We talked for a moment, the IT Manager told me not to let this experience stop me from working in the IT industry as he was happy to give me a reference. But I said it wouldn't as one of my older jobs had let me come back which he was happy to hear, so we shook hands on a good note then left.

What I said about an older job taking me back was an out and out lie. I said it because I didn't want to give anyone the satisfaction of thinking I would just be looking for another job. I knew what I had to do and this situation would never be duplicated again.

(*Self-Motivation Point: Never let your momentum or your belief in yourself drop no matter what the circumstance is. You are entitled to and of course will make mistakes along the road; the most important thing is that you learn from them and not let the disappointment consume you in any way, shape or form.*)

I wanted to prove that my spirit was not broken by what had happened which was why I handed my notice wearing a brand new leather Avirex jacket. It was my way of reminding myself that everything was going to be fine. During my journey home on the bus I had spotted the girl I had dated back in college as she was working for a retail shop that sold greeting cards, so I jumped off the bus and paid her a visit. She was surprised to see me! And because I had looked quite different to back in college, since having the newfound wealth (as short as that was for). My Avirex jacket would have given the appearance even more on how well I was doing. Even more to the point, I had dropped a tenner on the floor and could not find it! So I acted like it's OK I don't even need it, was only a tenner. She seemed to be impressed by it, but I don't know how I kept all this together and acting like nothing was wrong at the same time. But I wasn't going to allow the experience of what had happened earlier today to affect me – I will be back on top.

So I spent the next month and a half looking for a new role. It was an interesting battle, but it wasn't necessarily as tough as the last time, because this time I had another job on my CV. During my time at my last role, I was already being tantalized with different roles which were paying a lot more than what I was on. So there was some enticement for a new role too, which made it more of an adventure. A pressurized one but an adventure nonetheless. What made the search more pressuring was because of the responsibility I had on my shoulders. A couple of notable places in which I was interviewed were the Lord's Cricket ground, and a huge Law Firm situated down at Blackfriars. The Lord's cricket ground I thought I may have had an advantage because I was named after a cricketer (Jeffrey Dujon) but I was not into cricket at all. Ultimately I didn't get that role, but I really wanted it just so I could get my foot in the door. I could have learned to like cricket more if it meant I would get the position.

For the law firm I was so sure I had this, because it was another place I had the second interview at, and my first time doing an interview over a video conference. Unfortunately, I came close. But I didn't get it. Even though I went to a lot of interviews my spirit never really went down. But I know my mum had to financially hold us down at this point and even went a step further to pawn her jewellery just so she could keep us afloat. I told her, I'm getting this back for you, don't worry. She was very supportive and didn't care as long as I was good.

Eventually things started to look up more and more. I was studying even harder, my interview experience was even sharper and my knowledge of travelling around London was impeccable. I had scored an interview directly with the Sainsbury's head office in Holborn. I had gone to the interview and had a technical test both written and verbal with the interviewers and I remember them saying "That is impressive, Dujon!" Now I could finally see my time shining where I was getting that recognition in an interview I was looking for. And then on a late Friday night I was told I had got the job! Couldn't have been happier! And because it wasn't far before Christmas one of the benefits was 10% discount at Sainsbury's too! That was it, I could kick back and relax.

But then things got a little more interesting. Because my CV was so much more experienced, I was still getting the furious headhunting phone calls. And I still had calls for interview requests, some I accepted just for the sake of it though I had no intentions of taking them, and some I just tried to flat out ignore. But the Sainsbury's role that I thought was going to be my saving grace, started to change its shape on the offer. My understanding was that it was a permanent role, but then it had turned into a temp to perm role. Then when I reached out to the internal recruiter at Sainsbury's it turned into just a temp role saying "nothing is guaranteed in this world". But the end of the day I had an offer, but because it changed so much it made those other interviews stand out.

There was one interview that came up, and not knowing this one was going to change my life and career, I tried ducking and dodging the phone call for a couple of weeks, till one time I was walking home from an interview he got in touch with me, and said it was for a huge conferencing organization based in Chelsea & Kensington. At first I didn't really want to do it but then I thought why not, the agency was so persistent in it so I agreed. My mum always kept telling me, forget that interview, don't do it, you have an offer already. I tried to duck it but I said, "We know we've got another offer so we have nothing to lose". So, I made my way down to Chelsea, the first time ever being down the Royal borough of Chelsea and Kensington. The area alone was inspiring. I had a meeting with one of the interviewers who was the server support engineer at the time. One thing I remember was that he wouldn't smile for anything. And I tried my best and he almost did but not quite. So he took me to meet another server support engineer who was dressed like an aristocrat, who both quizzed me quite deep on technical questions. Aced it no sweat, overall it was a great interview and I took a liking to both guys, even if one of them wanted to keep a poker face. Even the building to me looked impressive. I always look around to see if I can picture myself working there.

The same day I had done an interview in Canary Wharf, South Quay – I had interviews all week in so many places. I was also negotiating the start date at Sainsbury's at the time to fit all my other interviews. I had then got feedback about the role in Chelsea, and they had were really positive and said I was invited to the second interview. Now I was always making the next stages now, I was getting so confident now!

It was tough to fit in because I had said I would start at Sainsbury's next Monday so I knew I would need to make a decision fast. So I did the interview at Chelsea on a Thursday. This was where I met the IT Manager. And also I met my match when it came to technical questions. At these times my technical sword was so damn sharp I was giving extra dialogue in my answers. Not necessarily being flash but I wanted to prove above and beyond my ability – this relates back to the Owner of the private institute where I did the course about the perception of when you fail an exam. The IT Manager was quite impressed at my age because I had only just turned 19 and saying I had one up on him because he first started at 22, so we had a good chat. But when the technical questions came, he fired a couple and he saw what I was doing. So he must have thought ok you want to be flash let's take it there. Then he asked me what's reverse DNS?

That wobbled me there at the time. I thought I knew it but I thought it may have been a trick question but he had me there. Taught me a lesson too. He did like the interview overall and knew I had another offer in the background. And he asked me when I wanted to hear feedback/decision and I said today! Think I was that confident I had it. Great talk and we shook hands and left.

Whilst on the bus back I had got a phone call in regards to the role I had interviewed for down in South Quay and they wanted me to attend an informal chat interview, which was basically an offer. See I had gone down to South Quay to do a technical test which you needed to pass at a high pass rate. And I managed to pass it and get an interview. But I really didn't want it because I had so many things going, and at the time I was more focused on the role in Chelsea as well as an offer in hand at Sainsbury's. And to make it more interesting it was a guy from the same agency as the guy representing me for the role in Chelsea. I hated these conversations so I tried to make up a story like I had no money to buy a ticket. But he saw right through it.

"Dujon, don't bullshit me. If you don't want to do the interview just say you don't want to do the interview."

I said, "Ok, I don't want to do the interview."

"But this role is a great role and doing all these projects."

Bit of a back and forth but I said had too many things going on as well as an offer I had already and waiting for the role in Chelsea's decision.

So he said, "So you're going to pass up this interview which would be an offer so you can wait for a role that you're waiting feedback from? Well I hope for your sake it really does come up because that's ridiculous."

At this point I was starting to get annoyed, I had a concrete offer, another which I knew I had and I simply didn't have space for another one. So then he said, "Dujon, we've got 45 minutes now till the interview – are you going?"

I just stayed silent. Then he said, "Ok don't worry I'll just let them know and cancel it...bye!"

Intense but it had to be done. I'm sure he knew his colleague had me for another role so I didn't understand why he was so adamant to steal it from him.

Later than evening, I remember I was watching the phone like it was going to change shape. Then I got a phone call for the role in Chelsea: "Dujon, you got the job!"

"Yes!!" Now I really was happy I had double said what I promised my mum. They had to get confirmation from the CTO in New York and that was okay too. I remember the agency ringing and I was away and my mum answered, and she thanked him for his hard work.

But the good news didn't stop there. The next day, all my other interviews I didn't even remember I had done...all came back as offers again!! And the best part was: all of them were at least £2000 more than I was earning in my previous role. So I had 5 offers now. But I had to let a few down, of course, which was never easy for me.

The Sainsbury's role I eventually let go, and the internal recruiter was not happy. She said "I'm very disappointed as you had committed to this temp role etc" but it had changed from perm to temp. The security in it was gone at that point, so I couldn't really accept now that I had multiple solid perm role offers.

But anyways, I had one week off and five new offers! And I had gladly accepted the role at Chelsea. Not bad a way to finish after just turning 19.

CHAPTER 12
– ROUND TWO

I started about some time in the middle of December, so it was like déjà-vu in terms of knowing another incomplete payslip was coming, but at least I was back in the game again. Going through the company induction really put me at ease, I could really see myself staying here for a long time which was the feeling I wanted. The IT Manager there was pretty encouraging and we had a conversation on my first day as a bit of a pep talk. He said, "If you mess up... actually let me change that, if you f*** up then it's best to come out with it so that it can be sorted rather than making a situation a lot worse. If you need help with something then ask me. If you ask me again that's absolutely fine, but if you ask me a third time then I'll start to get annoyed." Actually I appreciated not only the advice, but it was the way he delivered it to me. The directness gave me a clear understanding.

I did have a lot more of a determination to prove myself again but I was highly on edge in the first month. I remember I was tasked with troubleshooting a couple of managers' laptops which I had done correctly but they weren't responding to the fixes like they should, so the IT Manager at the time saw me working away, came over and said, "I can see you're working hard on them but I'm just a bit conscious about the amount of time it's taking." This only put me further on edge so he had a look with me. I can't remember what he advised me to do technically but I remember it was something I had done exactly and I belted out, "That's exactly what I did!" Showing my frustration at that point.

"Ok, OK relax!" he said.

The experience at my last role was still raw on me at the time, and as I was in the probationary period stage I had a hell of a lot to prove, so my key focus was to make absolutely no kind of silly mistakes whatsoever. The only way I could negate my "on edge" feeling was to keep my head down and just keep working. So for that month I remained quiet and to myself and just kept on top of the helpdesk calls coming in, and it was getting recognised that I was closing a good amount of calls. I had a couple of comebacks for incompleteness but the majority were handled first time.

The IT Manager then took me down to the server room to show me around the cables, switches, patching panels and port numbers and how they were patched in. He did a little memory test to see if I remembered, and it was a bit to take in at the time but I got it eventually. Christmas was approaching and it was the last day of the week before Christmas the following week so we were able to get our pay cheques from the finance department. At that time it was just under £800 because I started somewhat in the middle of December. Christmas then was a little bit rough financially but it was a good Christmas because I was back in the game, like I said I would be. Me and my mum did have a bit of a back and forth in terms of the payment I got because there were a lot of bills at that time and she wanted almost all of it. I tried to put my foot down to say it was going to be split 50/50, but I think I ended up making it about 80/20 in her favour as I didn't think I needed that much to make it through because I just needed lunch and that was it until the next year. When returning back to work after the Christmas period, they had a Christmas party at work and everyone was given a glass of champagne – of course they had to check my age because I used to look extremely young back then and only being 19. They had a Christmas party set up at the London Dungeons down London Bridge where everyone was dressed up as something kind of like a Halloween party. It was my first taste of any kind of festivities company-wise and I had an idea of what it felt like to be important, especially when I left and the security let me out saying "Have a nice evening, sir". That was different.

Now turning onto 2007, somewhat refreshed from Christmas, back into the field of proving myself again. Still maintaining and holding down the helpdesk calls, but this time I was now leading the call closure rate by a good mile. Starting to build a rapport with the different departments around the business. We had a meeting in their build room just to catch up about progress from everyone, and the IT Manager asked the server support guys what their feedback was of me and they said I was doing a great job, but just to make sure I fully finish the jobs that I started, which was fine and constructive.

During this period I had run out of the money from my share of the pay cheque I'd had last month, so I went back to packed lunches for that moment to get through. Then the IT Manager and one of the support engineer guys had organized for some guys to go paint balling. Which was free – I just needed £1 to pay for the 1000 allocated balls we were to have each. This was a great way to have a relationship outside of work too so of course I went.

But I was embarrassed that at that point I didn't even have a pound on me. I had a great time at the paintballing, but I had to borrow that pound from the Server Support engineer to pay for it because I had absolutely nothing at that time. I ended up losing my house keys at the same place too.

Back to the office now, the next week, the IT Manager had given me a huge task back then which was to build a directory of every staff member and take down each of their extension numbers. Now this building was huge, about 3 huge floors of staff, including their sister company who were also in the same building. Not only that, I had to go with the knowledge I had of the server room and patching panels. I had to trace each cable from their desk phone to the floor connection and note down the server port number and trace it from floor to floor down to the server room and note the correct patch panel number. Some staff members gave me a hard time because they refused to move or just flat out didn't want to talk to me, but this is where your customer service skills kick in. But after doing this all day I had a record of everything. I went a step further, typed it up, formatted it and sent it to the IT Manager. He must have given me the biggest amount of recognition I had ever gotten to date from that.

After a long January, I finally got my first full pay slip, and it was almost as big as the first one I got at my last role and this was just a regular month. Now you have to understand I was in Sloane Square/King's Road of all places, and for a young 19 year old to be getting that much back then and before the recession and pulling £300 out of the cash machine just to know how having £300 in the wallet felt like was huge. An indescribable feeling.

The motivation for a young guy like me was huge. I mean the Royal borough of Chelsea and Kensington? Working on King's Road with the big salary I was getting at the time? You just couldn't beat a motivation like that.

One of the most expensive areas I had ever seen at the time, and I was doing somewhat of a corporate job there and it was an amazing thing to experience. It can only motivate you to push more.

When I went out for lunch I sometimes used to work my way down from the bottom of Sloane Street/King's Road all the way up to the top of King's Road/Fulham Road. I started taking my walks to a slightly different level especially when it came to lunch time as I became a creature of habit visiting the Waitrose where they had the hot food, or it was McDonald's with the subway opposite of it but I grew very tiresome of it.

So I went on Google to try and find other places I could eat at...well, let's be honest Burger King, Nando's, all the good stuff. But the nearest ones were next to Gloucester Road Station. So I did it. I walked all the way from King's Road all the way down to Gloucester Road station. If anyone has done it you can understand that's a little bit of a distance. For those who haven't attempted it, then I welcome you to take the CHALLENGE! Because when I'm hungry I'm down for the walk.

CHAPTER 13
– WE'RE GONNA MAKE IT

After about a couple of months in, there was a huge explosion in one of the manhole covers next to the office and it took out a lot of the servers in the server room, which caused mayhem. I took the initiative to remain on the floors just to help out with anything technical as well as man the phones to communicate what was happening and what was being done to resolve it. As I wasn't that technically proficient when it came to servers, the IT Manager said I could leave at the normal time as he was going to take over and he pretty much stayed there throughout the night to sort it. I didn't leave straight away because I wanted to help more so I did what I could then eventually left, which he appreciated.

Things got back to normal, and a couple of weeks after that, was the dreaded probationary period meeting. Not going to lie, I was really nervous about this, second guessing myself as to whether I had done well enough and dwelling on the one time I didn't do this and that etc. I think I had started to build in a thought process of expecting the worst, so that was how I went into the meeting.

(*Self-Motivation Point:* Sometimes it is better to prepare for the worst or worse-case scenario. You'll find at times the unexpected can happen at any time. In this case my previous experiences installed a fear factor, but at the same time taught me to stay on my toes.)

So the IT Manager and I had a good talk about my performance and there was a rating system over various categories. How he shaped it was he asked me what I rated myself and then he would either agree or give me a rating he felt was correct. A lot of them I tried to put as excellent and the majority of them he agreed or said yeah you could do that. Some things I noted for improvement and he agreed because he wanted me to obviously rise up technically, to get more involved with other things and even projects. We briefly talked about when I first started. I remember him saying something like "I'm going be honest. When you first started I wasn't really sure if I saw you staying here much longer". That would have been because I was really on edge back then so I got it. "But then you kept your head down, got stuck in and you really performed" – so it was all promising at this point.

He also said that I needed to come out of my shell a lot more, which was something I was working on. We then caught up briefly on the status of the manhole incident and he was saying how tired he was from doing that but that's why they pay him the big money.

I remember asking him, "Is it all worth it for that big money?"

And he said, "Well, when you get the recognition and everyone in the business including the owners and managers personally thank you for everything you did...then yes it was definitely worth it". I really did learn a lot from him and definitely would note him down as an early mentor to me. He told me that once I was here I would be set for life, and it was 100% true. And that was concluded as me passing my probationary period and I was just elated at that point, finally got over. Well, maybe not got over but was able to overcome that obstacle of the probationary period meeting. What was so perfect in its timing was that it was payday the same day so it just took me to a different stratosphere of being happy that I got past this. I hadn't really spent anything from the last time I got paid so I really had a lot on me this time. I may have done this on purpose with the notion of not knowing what would happen. But eventually I started to indulge in the majority of the restaurants down King's Road for lunch, I ate in every restaurant in King's Road that exists from then till now including places that no longer exist now and I can name a good few. As promised, I got my mum's jewellery out of the pawn shop, put a few hundred in her pocket and all of the bills were in credit, plus some spending of course! Well to be fair at this point I had bought everything an average 18-19 year old would want and that list I made back in the work placement days was completed a long time ago. I took my mum to some huge restaurants this time mainly down King's Road. Also at this time I was more into seeing the colour of my money rather than spending it. At this point I was literally taking out £300 from the cash machine and had it balled up and just thrown lying around the floor at home. When my dad would visit he would just see balls of money everywhere, he was even more confused, he'd never seen anything like that. I was on a high but an accomplished high. Whilst I paint this image of flashness I'm not encouraging anyone to this exactly, but I had gone through a bit of a journey so I needed some kind of clownish boost, and that same money was put into a bank account and saved.

(*Self-Motivation Point: It does good for the morale to see some kind of materialistic purchase when you do gain a huge accomplishment, just a physical representation of a milestone you reach so you always have a reminder of the work you put in to get it.*)

I was almost making too much money for someone my age. At 19? I had bought everything I would have wanted so it was only logical to save it. That way I could do whatever I wanted...whenever I wanted and I was also paying the bills fairly too so I wasn't just pocketing the money. That...and also repayments for my CDL (Career Development Loan) I had taken out to pay for my private adult course were to start in a few months, which was about £120 a month so I was preparing for that. At that point as young as I was I took on the responsibility and mindset of a grown man. My frivolous spending was done at 18 on the first one or two cheques, but now I was preparing for the future and to ensure we would be good for life and that's more important than splurging money on useless things. My money stacked up quickly and even more when we used to get extra work which would involve us doing overtime from huge desk moves. This consisted of one of us project managing the move and moving all computers and phones from one floor to another and setting them all up again. A task which we had to do after-hours from 6pm and not finish until about 3-4am. As long as it was, the overtime I would get was huge! And because regular demands of this kept happening there was a period in which I didn't remember what my actual salary was! Money went straight to my savings and I just watched it grow in my bank book. Can you believe with all of this and my bank still didn't let me have a debit card!? Only a cash card where I could withdraw but nothing else. Course whilst it looks all like responsible thinking, my mum was in my ear to save money, and my dad was as well. I was never really spending crazy anyway, didn't really want much at this point. It's funny how your perception of life starts to change as well as things you experienced before are looked at very differently. For example, I remember when 50 Cent came out with the song "I Get Money" and it was huge at that time. But when I was listening to that song at the time now it wasn't just the beat or bars I was listening to, I was listening to it even more because it was true to me! The song just really was a great representation of how I felt at the time.

CHAPTER 14
– 1ST LINE TO 3RD LINE – REAL QUICK

My focus did not drop on my current role, in fact I was more motivated than ever now, I could relax and push on. I remember one time me and the rest of the team in the IT department were walking to lunch and we got on the topic about certifications and I had mentioned that I did have the A+ certification and the IT Manager responded saying "Yeah but I only care about that if you were just going to be opening up computer boxes". That statement made me re-evaluate my position in terms of where I stood in the food chain, and more certifications seemed like the next step to go, and also to get my revenge on the last exam which I had failed back when I was still working at my last role. Another driving force I had was when I was working in the server room doing some cable patching with a temp worker in the IT department, we were pretty much the same age. And then out of the blue he just said to me "You really need to step your game up."

I was like "Huh? What do you mean?"

He explained that I needed to step my game up in terms of getting up in the rankings where job titles and positions were concerned, maybe he must have seen that I looked content in the position I was in. And to tell the truth at that time I think I was. Maybe getting over the hump of the probation period may have made me not see a bigger picture already yet.

"I can imagine that amongst your friends you most probably are making the most, a ton of money. But compared to the rest of the guys you work with you are really bottom of the pile," he said. And let me tell you this, when I look back at this advice and even when I first heard this, this was maybe one of the best motivated pieces of advice I ever heard, and he was just under a year younger than me in fact. This set a fire for me to really look at where I wanted to be. Not jobwise but my overall career. So I immediately hit the books to study. Now that I had a job I wasn't going to study to the point I was losing weight the last time, but what I did do was study on lunch breaks and for an hour or so when I got home. I had a decent enough computer which had a virtual lab built where I could emulate what I read, but this time I also had the real-life scenario of my current role to back it with. Unfortunately I failed the exam again – I was quite close, but I was hugely disappointed. The server engineer I used to sit next to said he felt I took the exam a little too early. Even though I had practice exams I was using for Transcender and getting high marks. Maybe I should learn to pace myself more in the stamina of conditioning my revision. During this time the IT Manager had announced that he was leaving! It was quite a shock at the time especially to me, at that time he was like a mentor to me so it was strange to think of him going. I remember he called me outside to have a talk with him to see how I felt about it. I said I understood if he felt like he wanted a change, but I really respected that he even cared about my opinion and even kept me in the loop. I think this was the time he had said to me he was now going to go into contracting, at the time I kind of knew what this was but I didn't realise the market potential of it at all. I soldiered on and kept up with my revision and then I finally managed to pass my MCP Windows XP exam! It was the first Microsoft exam certification I had at 19. Also, the pass mark on these exams were significantly higher than the A+ 50% rate, these are are all 70%, so this required more focus from me. But finally I had another certification under me now and it hyped me up so much that I started to look for and investigate all of the other certifications, as I started to understand there were different certification paths, ones which I was already familiar with were ones like the MCSA (Microsoft Certified Systems Associate) and MCSE (Microsoft Certified Systems Engineer). The

MCSE certification I was amazed at because it was like the equivalent of a degree in the IT Industry at that time, and the fact it took a total of 7 exams to fulfil the overall certification, this was now the goal for me! After my first taste I wanted to build on my profile so I went for the next exam which was the MCP Windows Server 2003 exam, and I managed to pass that just before my 20th birthday, so I was happy I was building a little portfolio of certifications at this point. I had good support from the other members in my team as once I told them I had passed they communicated it across to everybody! I started to take on a target of doing at least 3 exams a year from then on, and I was paying for every single exam I took. This was how seriously I took my development. I always felt that you feel the dedication to the task at hand even more when it's your own money, so you can't afford to lose or make a mistake in every sense.

Meanwhile we had a new IT Manager start; he took time out to have a conversation with every one of us to get to know us and see exactly what we did in our roles. We got on quite well. During other conversations we had we talked about my career growth and what more I wanted to work on, to see more of, then eventually something of a pay rise got mentioned. Then again it could have been me that said it as a joke. I remember he said, "Tell you what. When you are resolving the issues and closing the calls, create a separate folder where you can collate all the Thank You emails or responses you get." It was an interesting strategy to have a justification for why I was worth the pay rise. It was perfect for me as I had a truck load of these before he even started so.

Taking into account what the temp worker had told me, I started to get more involved in some bigger tasks. Some involved configurations of servers and also building them from scratch using a RIS server (Remote Installation Service - for those who don't know this is trembling old), leading the upgrades from desktop machines from Windows 2000 to Windows XP as well as taking on the lead for doing the Laptop Encryption rollout. This may have been an early introduction for me being very thorough when it came to troubleshooting. See, this laptop encryption almost took a day to perform and used a password to unlock it during boot up, but the passwords never worked on any machine, which was mind boggling because it was confirmed multiple times it was correct. I had somehow stumbled on the issue. It was using a US keyboard only on that portion of the boot up. See, it wouldn't show any clear text so you would never be able to tell that was the case, but the recognition was great for me and also a relief.

But back to what the temp worker said about stepping my game up, bearing this in mind I had my new certifications ready to take on anything big but it never really came up. One time we had one of our regular monthly meetings so that we could realign the IT department and one of the topics was to establish what each person specializes in so that we had a go to person for each. There was one for Cisco, a couple for servers/infrastructure, but then when it came to me, the IT Manager said, "I think more hardware he specializes in."

"Hardware!?" I thought to myself. Because a lot of the helpdesk calls I had sometimes involved opening up machines, replacing them with new RAM or hard drive installs, but I was doing so much more technical tasks besides that. I understood what he meant but to me I hated that I would be the go-to person for that. To me no one was going to say hey Dujon does this RAM really go with this model of machine? Nope, don't see it, especially when we had multiple global offices. So I felt like I had to do something about this, so I went to look at the job boards, mainly JobServe just so I could really test my career profile as it stands now. I wasn't really looking for another role, to leave, but I wanted to prove to myself that I was more than just the go-to guy to replace RAM in an old PC. I don't really remember if I went to many interviews as such, I was a little bit more selective instead of perhaps flooding the market.

I had found one job that was for a field server engineer for a small managed services company, but it was for a 3rd line role. This would be a challenge as my role was primary 1st and 2nd line, but what I was studying and taking exams for was 3rd line knowledge so it would be interesting to see how this worked out. I sent my CV for this role and to my surprise they were interested in seeing me for an interview. I had studied and learned how to format my CV a lot more and made all keywords of relevant skills stand out in bold font as I had an educated guess that agencies were just looking for only those keywords, especially if they were not technical at all. So I had prepared for the interview and made my way down to South Quay, an area I had become quite familiar with in the past from previous interviews. The setting of where their office was really a sight to behold. Over the river banks and with a nice little cafe serving homemade food. After killing a bit of time here I made my way to the interview. To set the scene I was in about a mile long stretched boardroom with the table to match, with whiteboards, screens and projectors. Then 3 interviewers came in, and I knew this was not going to be any walk in the park. At first they were amazed by my age firstly, but then with that they thought there is no way he was technical enough for this. So they created some huge scenario based questions around server complexity, failovers on different sites, disaster recovery etc. Now bear in mind I hadn't even been touching any of this where I was working! So just my own book revision knowledge and my test labs, but I was able to answer everything and in quite intricate detail on everything they drew out and asked. They looked at each other in amazement and said ..."He's right!"

I thought to myself "I am!?...I mean yeah of course...I think!" They really pushed the technical boundaries on this, I think it may have been the best technical test interview I've had. At the time I applied for this role I can't remember what stage but probably on the initial phone conversation they asked me what salary I was looking for. Now I asked for what I felt at the time was an astronomical figure... to give a breakdown at the time I was on £20k and I asked for £28k. I didn't know or care if they were going to give that to me or not, as I just wanted to prove my technical ability after all the work I had put into myself.

One of the last questions that they asked me was "What inspires you? Do you have someone that you look up to?" I remember my answer being "Well I don't really have any role models as such that I look up to. I get inspired by many different things but I'm striving to be the person that others would want to aspire to be". They seemed to really love that answer so much that they wrote it down themselves!

The interviewers had stepped out for a moment, then they came back in and talked amongst themselves for a few seconds. Then they all turned their attention to me. And the main interviewer said, "Well Dujon. We've all discussed it and we've decided we are happy to give you what you asked for."

"What I asked for? I don't even know what that is. Can't be the money I asked for," I thought to myself.

I said, "Ok."

Then they said, "So that's the full £28k, plus a bonus, expenses and also a lunch allowance."

What in the world just happened!? I'm telling you I couldn't even fathom what I had just been told! I was not expecting this but I just made a miracle happen here! I played it so cool and said, "Great, well I would be more than happy to accept." Calm with no kind of backflips, front flips whatsoever. I shook hands with everybody with a confidence I never had before. Now just like in the past, I rang my mum's phone, off the hook once again, this time she answered with some quickness. I was on the DLR train at the time but luckily it was empty and I just went on one like "I GOT THE JOB! They want to give me what I was asking for they're giving me a bonus and a lunch allowance!" Being that I was a foodie beyond belief back then and had already consumed most of King's Road up to Fulham Road, so to give me an allowance to eat!? It's a done deal!

My mum said, "What did you ask for?"

"£28k!" I screamed out. Her reaction sounded like she almost wanted to cry. Couldn't make up this news, this was such an unexpected turn of events. I actually didn't really want to leave where I was at, but an offer like that would have made my career even bigger; forget the money, I had so much of it coming out of my ears, what you get paid is the experience you gain for your career. It was a field type role so would have had exposure to all kinds of organisations and huge experiences.

The hardest part was to come, which was the notice period. I had never done this before and had no clue how to approach this, so again I called on my mum to help me with this. She had some kind of speech or structure for me as a template I could use to explain what I had been offered and why you are thinking of taking it. It was approaching Christmas so I had to make a decision quick so I sent a short message to the IT Manager on Skype and asked him if he had a few minutes. We got together and met in the build room. I had explained I had another offer and that I was thinking of taking it. He then had a look of worry and then he took his glasses off to rub his eyes. Priceless moment, I thought that I could provoke a reaction like that meant I added value. We spoke about the role itself I was being offered and that I wanted to work on bigger things and didn't feel I was getting exposure to that where I was, and the role I was offered was a 3rd line role. He responded saying that he felt like I was a little bit raw for 3rd line. It's funny because that's what I had thought, but after proving myself I no longer agreed with it. I explained I was in a tough position because I really didn't want to go, and he didn't want to see me go. Of course the salary was a big shock too. He told me that he was actually going to give me a pay rise anyway from £20k to £25k because he thought my salary was way too low for me. The confidence inside me as well as the huge jumping up and down feeling continued on. How we left it was I said let's catch up after lunch and I'll have a think.

I went to lunch and thought about big decisions like this the only way I know how, over a huge meal consisting of a steak! I rang my mum and explained the conversation I'd just had. She had come up with the genius idea of asking them to match my offer. So after lunch I grabbed him again and said I'd thought about it, and if we can raise the salary to the same as I had been offered then I would stay. About an hour or so went by and we caught up again and he said yep that's fine. I think it was for the best I did this – the offer I had was brilliant and I knew what I was capable of, but I felt like I needed to define myself a bit more and I had only been at this job for a year at the time.

Though I did get the salary rise, and also was eligible for a 3% bonus (strange number but more money is more money) there was a condition that came with it. I had to be contractually bound to stay there for at least one year and if I left I had to pay the money back. No problem for me anyway.

So I had achieved an immense amount, 2 new exam certifications, a job offer, a job counter offer with a an 8k pay rise, 3% bonus and was already pending an overtime payment all before Christmas in 2007. Well we've all had worse days.

CHAPTER 15
– HOW DO YOU DEAL WITH IT?

I had faced my fair share of disgruntled members of staff. Some had frustration because of their own workloads, you have to become thick skinned quite quickly at times and it's sometimes a skill which is difficult to learn when young. I remember one time we were in the middle of a desk move and I was given a task to sort out the laptop of the managing director of the sister company. Something about the laptop kept constantly crashing. At first he was ok but then all of a sudden he just flipped on me, being impatient on the actual fix whilst I was trying to understand what was going on. "What is taking so long, you not done yet!? Do I need to get the other guy!?"

I remained calm and just tried to re-assure them that I was trying to investigate the problem whilst he was pacing up and down the office. One of the server engineers walked past and asked me if I was ok. I said yes but I really wasn't, but I wasn't about to let this situation get to me so I proceeded to look into their laptop. One moment their Microsoft Outlook application had crashed, which I went to re-open and it had a display message saying that the program had not been closed down properly and was entering into a safe mode.

"It wasn't closed properly. Why wasn't it closed properly?" he said to me. I explained that the application had closed itself because it was frozen and had to terminate the program, and that it was normal if a machine does lock up from maximized resources, but he wasn't necessarily trying to hear that explanation. "I've had this laptop for 2 years! And it's never done that!" he said.

As I was telling him step by step what I was trying to do, mid conversation he just stared at me then just walked out of the office. He came back a minute later and then wasn't even listening to me anymore. The other server engineer came in to take over and help so I didn't have to keep looking at his laptop anymore. It was embarrassing for me, you never know how to really deal with those situations. Sometimes it's just part of the territory, especially when you are front of house for your IT department. It's all a part of shaping your customer service skills. You don't always deal with happy clients or customers, it takes a good amount of diligence to be able to put up with irate clients or customers as well. But this managing director had a reputation for having these kind of outbursts. So much to the point that he only dealt with one specific server engineer. One reason being he was the only one he trusted, which worked for everyone else because anytime they rang, everyone would literally pass it straight to the server engineer he entrusted. Whenever I answered to him he would ask for every other staff in the IT team before he would even ask me for any kind of help.

Another time when the owner of the company was also having trouble with some kind of access which was restricted to his laptop, and I guess he had been dealing with other team members as I was not aware of what was going on with this. I was assigned a ticket to go and assist them with what they needed. But little did I know I was entering a line of fire.

As soon as I got up to the floor and approaching the office, he marched out of the office and started screaming at me. "Why would you tell me that it's working when it's not!? I've been trying all day to get this to work after YOU said it was fine and it's not F******** working!"

I didn't even know when he was talking about. It wasn't me he spoke to. And he did it in front of everybody on part of the HR and Finance department.

When you're part of a team sometimes you have to take the blame as a whole, and not be surprised if it comes at you individually. I represented the IT department so I took the screaming. It's easy to be outraged and complain but that's too easy, and wouldn't accomplish much for how I deal with these situations. Just had to grin and bear it. Eventually you build up thicker skin and try to understand the positions of the staff members and the part they play in the business and how their frustration and their target can be crossed together.

Not only can we face odd situations inside the office but also outside too. A very interesting moment I had was one time after work. I was waiting for the bus to go home, and just to paint the picture there was a bus stop which was only for one bus and that was on Draycott Avenue. Very huge houses on this street, mansions in fact. On my daily commutes I would get off the bus on the same road and walk through to the office so I could admire all the different houses and private terraces. This only expands the mind for me as a physical representation of what I could have if determined enough.

But back to the story. Whilst I was waiting for the bus, I saw two police officers who were patrolling the area for some odd reason, never seen them before but it looked normal, I guess. So, they walked up real slow heading towards me and I wondered in the back of my mind if they were going to talk to me. But then they just walked past me and I thought nothing of it. Whilst I turned around just looking around the houses I turned around slowly...and the same two police officers were in my face! About two inches away from my face.

"Alright!?" one of them said.

"Yes," I replied back.

They already had somewhat of a confrontational look on their face so I already had it in my mind this was going to be some kind of interrogation for who knows what.

"What are you doing here?" the policeman asked.

I was just confused, saying to them, "I'm waiting for a bus."

"There's no buses that come down here," the policewoman said to me almost immediately after I said that, damn near cutting me off.

Okay? Now I'm even more baffled because I replied back saying "the bus stop is over there" and we were standing right next to it. And I also pointed to another one which was exactly opposite the street. They looked at it, each looking and feeling stupid as they paused for a few seconds, not giving a quick response like they had done before but they were both still inches away from my face. After staring at me for a few seconds my phone rang and it was my mum. I didn't really want to answer it whilst they were in my face but then the policeman said, "You going to answer that!?"

So I answered it, spoke for a moment telling her I'd call her back then I put the phone down.

In retrospect I should have said the police were talking to me. I wasn't scared but I wasn't entirely sure what was going to happen at this point, especially when Draycott Avenue is normally quiet at times with little to no people there. Whilst I was on the phone they were still in my face.

"Where are you coming from?"

I told them I was finishing from work, told them the name of the company and the address of it since they were in doubt of what I were saying. But they seemed to understand I really was just finishing work as they had a station not far from where I work.

The policeman responded saying, "Ok, sir, we are sorry about that, it's just because you had your head down and were standing around. And there have been some robberies around the area as of late and we have to stop anyone we find suspicious." Ok...so I was wearing a suit and waiting for a bus I can see how that can arouse suspicion, which was what I was thinking at that time. They took my details down so they could make a report and said I can pick it up at the station if I wanted a copy. I should have picked this up. I don't know who would be insane enough to try and rob a house in this area of all places, they had security alarms that probably rang officers that would shoot you on sight, so I never understood why or how I provoked some kind of fear or suspicion.

But here is the irony about this story. The next day there had been a huge story on the news about a solicitor or a judge who was shooting at their neighbour from his bedroom window with a shotgun in King's Road! I wonder if he had his head down looking suspicious. To be fair he probably did, he needed his head down in order to aim.

*(**Self-Motivation Point:** You have to keep your cool no matter what the situation is. The moment you panic is the moment your rational thinking just stops. I don't know as to why they would have stopped me for looking suspicious, but I made them understand that I was nothing what they thought I was.)*

CHAPTER 16
– ENTREPRENEURIAL SPIRIT

I had started looking at ideas for a business just for a fun experiment. Again, no expectations. From the experience I had gained and from some market research, I had looked at an idea of combining multiple parts in a business into a consolidated IT Consultancy powerhouse.

There were a lot of IT training and IT Solutions companies as well as Consultancies. So I had an idea of what if I could have an IT training division which would teach IT industry courses similar to what I did on my private course. And on completion of the courses they would then be able to be enrolled into their first IT role in the IT consultancy side of the business where they would gain real experience with having a managed service helpdesk with field engineer requirements where needed. The IT consultancy would have multiple tiers from helpdesk to architects so it operated as a fully functioning consultancy as well as a training division that would be able to get fresh talent such as people my age and have them in the IT industry. The company would also have an IT Recruitment agency side which would be able to source candidates to clients like a normal agency, but also scouting for potential students to enroll onto the training courses and the possibility of being hired as well as for the internal IT consultancy.

I had put a business plan together and had put a copyright to the initial idea. Of course I started to understand patents but may had been slightly over my head at the time thinking the copyright of the initial idea was enough, but I was getting there. I didn't know of how the process worked on where to pitch a business or business plan and through more research I came across the Angel Investments network which I had signed up to, and created a profile based around the business idea. And what happened next, I did not expect. The amount of interest that I got was insane. About 20 investors had got in touch with me left, right and centre all around the world. I remember the admin of Angel Investments got in touch with me and said, "This is the most attention we've ever seen on here for a business idea. Never seen this amount of interest in a business before." It was a great achievement but came with immense pressure. Quite a few wanted me to pitch the idea to them personally as well as explaining the business plan and pitching online which resulted in offers which were between £10 - £25 million. This was huge for me. But the concern I had was that I had really no financial capital to invest in for myself. And perhaps the reality of the situation was though I had a great idea the road it could lead to where an investor would put 100% in, I could potentially have nothing as well as the stress of having a business and failing with someone else's money. I just didn't feel I was ready to take on an opportunity of that magnitude. Being 20 years old and though I'd done quite a bit I was very green to this area of business and decided to step away from it. I knew I needed a lot more experience in life as well as business before I could commit to something this big. Who's to say that I wouldn't return to this idea ? You can never tell how the future would pan out. But it was a great little look to see how it could be as well as bring in my 21st birthday.

CHAPTER 17
– WHAT'S THE NEXT MOVE?

We got so cool in the IT Department we started to play jokes on each other; of course when it came to practical jokes I only did these in self-defence. Once you play one on me you will face torment!

I remember two specific ones I used to do. One was to the server engineer I sat behind and he used to sometimes type his username and password wrong so I took advantage of this because he used to really show his frustration at it. Now I wasn't being cruel as he started this back and forth. So I used to remotely connect to his machine from time to time and when he tried to login I would type some extra characters in and when he tried to login it kept saying wrong Username or password. He used to do it so many times it used to hang for several minutes then fail or even be locked out. He damn near used to try to break the computer and start slamming the keyboard and mouse. He would ask me to login on his machine with the same credentials and it worked. He was really confused. Then when he logged out and tried it again, I did the same thing and it failed and he used to go ballistic! I must have done this once every two weeks, it was some of the funniest things I ever saw I was in stitches just watching it.

Another one I did, which was quite low key and no one could figure this one out, so for those who see this it was me! I had downloaded a piece of software that used VOIP (Voice over IP). I don't remember what it was called but it was free. You could ring all of the phones for free, but one cool feature it could do was make phones ring each other so I thought hmmm this could be interesting. So as a test I made a couple of phones ring each other in the Department I was working in; it used to confuse them as to how it even happened, thinking why did you ring me?

Then I took it a step further. I made the server engineer's phone get a phone call from Domino's pizza. So he answered thinking it was someone who had a technical issue whilst Domino's was trying to take an order. What was funny was that they were on the phone for over a minute and I'm thinking how no one has figured out who they are talking to!? Then eventually he put the phone down just looking confused saying Domino's pizza rang him. It was funnier being there but at that time it was hilarious. I had a few people ring him, I can't remember from the top of my head but they got more and more ridiculous.

But back to business, I had pushed on with two more exams which allowed me to obtain my first big certification – that was the MCSA (Microsoft Certified Systems Associate). Even better because I had it all done and dusted before my 21st and getting these certifications at the youngest age I possibly could would only elevate me in the best way. I did do an occasional interview here and there just to test myself. Sometimes you have to know your worth and need to challenge yourself in the market to assess your baseline, see where you stand. You can't always leave it to an organization to recognize your ability or potential, you have to take advantage of it, too.

After being at my job for two years now, I started to feel that I was being kept at the 1st line level a bit too much. I was already doing 2nd to even 3rd line type of tasks being thrown at me and started to grow tiresome of some of the day-to-day tasks. Some people used to call with…let's call it how we see it, ridiculous calls. Some used to call and say my mouse is on the right side and I want it on the left. Or that the printer doesn't work and it's because no paper was put in it. I could just feel my patience running thin with wanting to express myself on a more technical basis. The last straw for me, was when I was carrying out a desk move and someone had a pair of brown stained underwear just left there. That was it, I couldn't do it anymore, something had to change.

As it turned to 2009 my mission was to actually start looking for a new role for real this time, no practice. I don't really remember having a multitude of interviews but there was one notable one and one notable one only, which was a direct role and this was with an IT solutions company, who were a recruitment, training and solutions company at the time. The role they had advertised was perfect, it was for an Infrastructure Architect Specialist. I was really obsessed with job titles and this one just had success written all over it. I just had to get it.

In the past I always never really considered the travel distances in some roles. Again the hunger to progress had me overlook certain details and in this case this role was based in Wimbledon. And I hate underground trains! But I had no choice in this case so I took the district line down to Wimbledon during lunch time. First thing I do when I get to the area is check out how many places I can eat at. But after I analysed this I went into the building. It was a nice looking building with the inside being an atrium design. Also a computer gaming company was based in that same building and I still hadn't really let go of my games I was into at the time. So this interview consisted of the IT Manager and IT Service Delivery Manager. I had so much confidence at this point I had the ability to turn it to an interesting conversation; it's also great to squeeze a couple of laughs in where you can, too. After about an hour or so they brought in the Senior Engineer to have a little chat to me and we got on great. They were working on a lot of Virtualization technologies such as Hyper-V and this was essentially the first time I had heard of or got exposure to the System Centre technologies which I specialize in now. They were using SCOM (System Center Operations Manager) and SCVMM (System Center Virtual Machine Manager).

The interview was over and I made my way back to the office, I remember checking in with my mum saying to her there is no way on the planet that I won't get this job! Not sure what made me so confident but maybe I started to pick up a flare of knowing how to interview well and assessing how they perceived me. I guess the Achilles heel of my age started to work more in my favour now. Shortly after, the IT Solutions Company rang to give feedback on the position. Although I had all the confidence in the world, nevertheless I got nervous about hearing the outcome, wondering if I was going to be proven wrong in my thinking. But I was proven right: I got the job! At this time I still hadn't shaken off the screaming out yes! Though eventually this would die down but not today!

Now, I had to approach the hard part again, having the conversation about my notice which I really just hated. So I did it the best way which was to have a conversation with the IT Manager about my job and where he saw it going in the future because I had wanted to see if there were any plans at all on promoting me or having me become a more senior person. He said, "I can throw more tasks at you in terms of more 3rd line stuff but for the foreseeable future you role is most likely not going to change."

That really gave me enough justification to finally move on so I said, "Well in that case I've got another role offer which will allow me to get to where I need to, so I'm going to take it." Wow! I thought to myself that was real firm laying it down like that. But the IT Manager understood and went ahead and started the process of my notice.

I did have a slight moment of panic, because I had signed and sent back the signed contract for my new role but they never received the paperwork. So I started to get concerned and emailed the HR there to find out what was happening and they were just as confused.

So I explained to the IT Manager the issue and he agreed for me to go down there and get it signed. So I had agreed with the HR at my new role to go down there and sign the paperwork.

And just as I was about to get to the station, I got an email from them saying they had just received it! It had got delayed because of a shortage of 10p on the postage. Really!? 10p could have put me in bad situation I thought!?

When it was announced I was leaving, I had a very good response with a lot of great wishes and handshakes. I'd forgotten at this time I had been there for about 2 and a half years, seen three Christmases there too, so I had put in quite a bit of time.

But the time was right for me to finally move on. I had a clear vision on where I wanted to be and this was the next perfect step for me. I was still saving a good amount of money, I had multiple Microsoft certifications and a CV that was growing page by page, I felt strong.

I managed to get some downtime before I had started the role which was great for me to reset my batteries.

CHAPTER 18
– UNDERSTANDING YOUR WORTH

Now here we go. The new start with a brand new role which I was extremely proud of. Especially its job title.

I went through my induction and meeting the rest of the team and another chat with the IT Manager who was normally based down in Manchester but he came down for the sake of me starting that day. We had a conversation as part of the on-boarding. He said, "It was just a quick word to say we appreciate your accepting the role and starting with us. We had a lot of people for this role that we interviewed, but you clearly stood out." This IT Manager really gave me my first bout of "pure confidence" that I have carried around till this day because you don't realise the impact or skill you have sometimes. Even though it's important to hear that, and on the first day was even better.

Later on in my induction I had learned about the benefits system which was something called flexible benefits where we could buy and sell holiday days, adding healthcare/dentalcare and many other benefits. Now I had never heard of anything like this, and I started to hound the HR department for the login for this. I admit when I get like this I become really annoying...especially if I'm awaiting feedback for a job. I know the agencies are most likely chasing more than me... but to be honest when I'm in that mode I don't care.

Everything was going great so far, but I have to say this was the first time I was thrown in the deep end this deep and this quick! So to summarise there were the following projects kicking off.

Design and implementation of Dynamics AX 2009, Design and Implementation of OCS 2007 (Office communications server – for you young guys you now know this as Skype for Business) and also the Design Implementation of SCOM 2007 R3 and SCVMM 2008. Now...I'm up for a challenge as much as anybody but this was insane! In fact my first day I was already in design meetings with an external consultancy who were also part of the delivering of the projects. The timing of me starting there was impeccable as the IT Manager had gone on holiday the following week, as did the Senior IT engineer. So it was just me ...no kind of support or backup, I literally had to hold everything down. Of course this didn't stop my absolute panic at the time. Especially when project managers and architects were coming out all over the place with other things which were already in the pipeline before I started. And they were handing me deadlines on things I had no clue about. One time I came back from the toilets and I just saw a queue of architects and project managers literally just waiting at my desk. I saw them and watched them, but didn't come back to my desk because I really didn't want to have to face and put up with all of them all over again. Eventually they gave up and left a note for me to get back to them. I had left messages with the IT Service Delivery Manager to let him know what was going on as he was really the only person who could advise about this situation, so he managed to get in touch with them to lay off me until the actual IT Manager came back from holiday. Whilst that had been silenced for that moment, I still had the daily project board meetings for the Dynamics AX 2009 project which also included an AD (Active Directory) Design using Windows Server 2008 R2. This was one hell of a learning experience and I had to remind myself this was what you wanted. You wanted to do more infrastructure, you didn't want to do anymore helpdesk duties or moving someone's mouse from the left side to the right side...well now you've got it. So, embrace it or drown. And that's what I did, embrace it!

*(**Self-Motivation Point:** Being thrown in the deep end can be the best way to soak up knowledge, but it can also be a pitfall especially if you allow yourself to drown in the situation you are in.)*

I got really involved and contributed a lot to the design meetings we had and managing my project tasks assigned to that particular project. Time flew at this point and I had a grip on everything and I was a lot more relaxed. So much to the point that once the IT Manager had come back from holiday I hadn't even worried about the situation I was facing in my first two weeks. Following that the Senior IT engineer came back from his holiday and everything started to go back to normal without the immense pressure I was facing. I knew that everything I had available project-wise to me was an absolute goldmine. I remember I had Skype installed and I used to talk to some of the guys I knew from my secondary school/college days. I was speaking to a couple of them and when I told him what I was doing workwise and what salary I was on they responded saying "WHAT!? How is that possible? What experience do you have?" I don't think they really understood at that point I had about 3+ years of work experience. And because I literally went straight out of college into a job in about 6-7 months, the transition is pretty quick! Considering the fact the friends I was speaking to were still in Uni. So thinking about it that is such a quick time to be in a role such as what I had and the salary to be on at 21!? Unbelievable at those times. Also at the time my salary (although it was 5k more than my last job) was almost a pay drop considering the overtime we were getting at the time. But this was better because it meant I got somewhat a close amount with no overtime to put in.

As much as I gained great success at such a young age, I felt there was a slight sacrifice at hand. Because I had gone so high up career-wise in just under 3 years, I had already made enough money to the point where I had bought everything I would have wanted back in 2006. I never experienced university in terms of the lifestyle the students had, so it's like part of the last bits of your teen years where you would do all kinds of stupid stuff. That had to be put on hold as I was building my career. Friends I used to hang with that constantly used to come to my house almost daily grew distant. Probably because our paths were diverging, as where I was career-wise my mentality changed from perhaps the average 21 year old with little to no responsibility. I was covering all household bills from the beginning of 2008 because I wanted my mum to retire and no longer work anymore. The recession had hit at that point and almost everywhere had an immediate impact with so many people being laid off left, right and centre, with my mum included. One time, we saw that the same supermarket she worked for was launching under a new brand, and they were doing a mass hiring event, which was great for people who didn't have a job, but it meant everyone who worked there in the past had to re-apply for all of their jobs back. They held an event in the Hilton Hotel and what I witnessed was the most horrific sight I ever saw. There were recruitment staff standing in certain areas of the hotel suite where almost 40 people per person were surrounding them. I told my mum to stand back whilst I looked at what was going on. I realised the recruitment staff had application forms, but what the staff did caused damn near an animal-like reaction. They started throwing application forms in the air, and the herds of people were jumping in the air, scrambling for the forms and pushing each other and stepping on each other. I thought to myself hell no is my mum doing this! So we went home and I told her you are not doing this, forget working again, I will take care of everything from now on.

So I had real grown responsibilities which I wanted to accept as well as building for myself also. Contrary to belief with the amount of interviews I had, I really didn't focus or care about the salary too much at all. It's important to obtain your worth, but a bigger salary is a short term relief, whereas a role that challenges you, gives you experience which is invaluable and is current, then that's the better long term benefit.

So back to my role, my probation period was coming up. Even though I wasn't worried at all, I was still anxious to get through it. I had worked pretty hard on this role, the most challenging 3 months on a technical aspect. I had got the designs implemented for Dynamics AX 2009, the new AD was built, I had implemented SCOM 2007 for the first time with the whole environment being monitored and implemented and SCVMM 2008 R2 which managed all of the Hyper-V physical hosts for the software development team, all while the Senior IT Engineer and I worked on getting the OCS 2007 working. We had a task to get it where you can call externally from your desktop machine to a mobile phone and landlines, and have them ring our desktops as well. These projects are the foundation of my career experience right now!

On the day of the probation period, as the IT Manager came to grab me for the meeting, an Architect came up to me and shook my hand.

"Well done, Dujon, great work."

"What for?" I said smiling but confused.

"The OCS 2007 is working! Internal calls and external calls!"

Wow! Not just the fact that everything was working but the timing of being told this on the day and exact moment of going to my probation meeting. Safe to say that went very well and the IT Manager actually gave me some great praise I still remember even to this day. He said, "Me and another guy were actually talking about you on the way to the office on the train. You actually don't know how good you are. The work you have done here in just 3 months is excellent! And you even got the OCS working as well, which is brilliant!" I couldn't have been prouder of myself at this point. So much of the negative experiences I had before were long gone and so far behind. Not to mention I was still putting in my 3 exams a year strategy and the certifications list was just getting bigger and bigger for me and I was still paying for them out of my own money.

I remember shortly after that time several new gadgets were released on the market, being the new PSP, the new Call of Duty with a limited edition Xbox Console and a Guitar Hero game with the limited edition Eminem/Jay-Z mix CD. I bought all of them the same day! Why? Well why not I used to think. This was when I felt the power of myself back then from how well I was doing. Back and forth on my journeys on the trains I had my ears always plugged into music, and one album I came across during my time at the new role was the Birdman – Priceless album. At that point that album changed my perspective in life in terms of the goals I had. At the time I was starting to feel contempt again in my position. Everything was going perfect. I had a challenging role and the salary to match and at the age I had it all. I almost felt like there wasn't really much else I could do at that point. But when I heard that album, and the lifestyle Birdman was talking about, it made me envisage more of what I could achieve and showed me there was a lot more I hadn't even seen or accomplished yet. It influenced me to want to take things to the next level.

I did start to pick up a different kind of attention after a slight accidental, maybe not accidental but misinterpreted. See, one of the other technologies I brought in was a tool called MDT (Microsoft Deployment Toolkit) which was able to install operating systems on machines over the network and can be done in an automated fashion. Now I had created some offline media on USB sticks so that other remote offices can build machines. Here is where the attention and misinterpretation came in. See, I had got so advanced with the configurations of building machines I could give the process a name, so just for testing purposes I called it "Dujon's Magic Stick" as USB sticks were being called magic sticks on some brands. So...once it was shipped across to other offices it went to the office in Manchester where I heard the majority of the staff were mostly women. So on approximately 100 machines being built was a message across the screen saying "Dujon's Magic Stick"! Wasn't exactly the way I planned to be known, but there was demand for me to come to the Manchester office after that!

Now turning to 2010, things were still cruising at my role. But I had seen that the big projects we had all at once were really the meat of the role, as things quietened down and times where we weren't really doing much but just maintaining service. BAU (Business as Usual) support is just as important, in fact more important, but I just felt not as motivated when it came to these moments. At the time a lot of the helpdesk duties and calls were being outsourced to another managed services company at the time. I had heard that a lot more was going to be outsourced to them. This really concerned me because we were already quiet and with that happening on top of it, I felt like maybe it was time for me to start searching for my new challenge. I did look for a little minute, but I had managed to gain the interest of two organisations for great roles. One I had found was through the Recruitment side of the private course I did. The client was a Japanese IT Solutions company. They had some great projects going on and it would have not only been great to snag that opportunity but would have been even better to have gotten it through the same place I did my course! All the times I had found other jobs I did it so quickly that the recruitment agents didn't get a chance to find a role for me, my demand literally took on a life of its own.

During this time I had created a LinkedIn profile to display my credentials on a wider scale, hoping to see if it would create an impact. Shortly after I was contacted on there about a huge IT consultancy that specializes in Microsoft technologies and were part owned by other massive technology giants. This was for a consultancy role and a huge amount of growth for me that was perfect for what I was seeking.

For the Japanese consultancy I did the first interview and I got on great with the managers; that followed on with great feedback with an invitation to a final stage interview. Then also I had to go through a pretty deep technical test with the other consultancy on a phone interview. It was pretty tough, but I managed to get through and prove great technical knowledge and that turned into a final stage interview as well.

The dilemma I had? Well both interviews were on the same day. I hadn't done two interviews in the same day for a little bit after being at my last role in Chelsea for almost 3 years. This was going to be one hell of a day to plan for, I thought! But after everything I had faced over the years and recently with the pressure at first starting at my new role? Bring it on!

So I had organized for the second IT consultancy interview to take place in the morning. One thing that got me excited about the prospect of working there was that it was in the West End! Imagine that being in the West End where your office is and unlimited amount of shopping and eating! Not to mention a Hummingbird cake shop next door. But back to business. Before the interview kicked off, they had sat me in a boardroom where I had to take yet again another technical test; this time it was paper-based. I looked at the questions and thought damn! This is quite comprehensive. But then again, bring it on! I was doing 3 exams a year so this wasn't going to scare me. I used some of my technical cockiness to add more extra detail to every answer. Certain ones I had no clue of, but I did my absolute best to try and know everything, being how I was then. After that was done the actual interview had started. It was a great way to understand the company, the working life, structure and of course the role which I would play. In the interview it was mentioned that there would be some form of travelling but I wanted to clarify exactly what this meant. I had no intention of travelling all four corners of the Earth, but I was reassured that there was only travel where necessary and the majority would be local, which I was happy with. This role was absolutely perfect for me, just for the fact I could be part of a company owned by some huge technology players and have a recognized specialization of some sort. It was a dream to be part of something like this. After that interview was completed, I went back home to get ready for the final interview at the Japanese IT consultancy which was a little later in the evening, so I had a bit of a break in between.

Now what I liked about this organisation was the working culture they had, the projects which they had kicking off, and also because it was actually next to the building where I did my course! So it was familiar surroundings and the place where my career was born – Liverpool Street. Side note – they were also paying more but it wasn't really about that. Though it was handy. I had met the overall IT Manager and we had an interesting conversation about my experience and some of the projects I had done at my current role and I was put on the spot to do a mini presentation or diagram of the design I did. It was interesting because this was the first interview I did where a presentation was required and on the fly. I had a couple of interview requests in the past where it was required to do a presentation before the interview, but I flat out refused them. My theory was that it was just another reason or angle to just tell you why you didn't get the role and it felt it was a way to gauge who you were more to use it against you. Or then again, maybe I shied away from it because of the feedback I had had in the past about my presentation skills. Maybe, but either way I didn't do them. But overall that interview went very well. I felt great about myself that evening that I had knocked two final stage interviews out the park on the same day.

I had no clue as to who I would have gone for if both offers came through. Initially I was adamant on choosing the Japanese IT consultancy for reasons of the travelling aspect with the other role, that I was still unsure of its certainty of being local, and also because I was still attached to the area and that the institute that I done the course at had got it for me. Already assuming the best at this point. But the second IT consultancy was offering exactly what I needed which was the most important in the long term. Ultimately I thought it would be an easier decision if only one of them turned into an offer, to kind of make my decision for me as I really couldn't have decided one over the other at that point. I decided to call my dad to get his opinion. Also at this point I just wanted him to feel like he was a part of something in my career as he had really missed or been absent from all of it besides the remark of me getting to where I was at now was impossible. I explained the two options and both roles, and broke it down to the good points of each.

"Well what I'm hearing is that you don't want to travel," he said. Which was really my main concern. Because something in me felt like the travel aspect was going to be more than what I initially thought. My dad's way of thinking was if there was something I didn't want to do and there was something that didn't require me to do it then choosing that role would be considered the "easy option". I think a lot of cases this is true. A lot of people avoid a challenge that becomes part of a great opportunity and run away from it. But I can assure you this wasn't really the case as I knew that if I didn't like the travel aspect then the job would also go down the drain, so it was more about making a careful decision. But as I thought about it during the conversation we had, I had decided to go with the role at the second IT consultancy if it came up. If the travelling part wasn't as bad then career-wise it was going to be the better option overall.

First up, second IT Consultancy feedback in and just as I thought – an offer was on the table. I was very happy with this because I was really tested technically to see if I was there or not. Not to mention I was told an Architect did the same test I did that day and we got the same score. Wow! I must have really been good. I THINK!

So now with that done, I'm patiently waiting for the next one now. And the phone rings and here it comes! I didn't get the job. I was a bit confused as to why!? I know I did perfectly. I was almost told I had it on the day, so I wasn't sure what happened. But apparently the projects or the budgets had fallen through and therefore my role was affected. In this unforeseen development there wasn't really anything I could do. It was sad because actually I was hoping for that offer the most, which told me that I most likely would have taken that role in the end. But it wasn't a bad outcome – I had an offer which would provide me with the perfect platform. So all in all, it was still a successful outcome but being me I wanted the gusto.

As a little time went by I ended up receiving the contract. It detailed the travelling aspect of the role which was noted as a 50 mile radius within London. That didn't seem too bad at all, but I started to have some second thoughts because I still really did like my current role. Something in me had some serious doubts about taking the role. I'm not sure if it was the uncertainty I had on the travelling, or maybe after everything I had experienced in the past I didn't want to rock the boat and be in another turmoil-like situation. So at one point I contacted the agency and told them that I was thinking of turning down the role.

"Well if that's how you feel I'm not going to waste my time etc etc," he responded. His response kind of made me question my doubts as he re-emphasized the opportunity that I would have been letting go, so from then I had changed my mind and decided to accept the offer. Maybe I was being silly; perhaps. Maybe I was potentially running away from something great. We will see.

Again it was very tough for me to hand in my notice. I really hated these conversations, but it had to be done. I spoke to the manager about me having another role and where I saw myself going career-wise. He understood where I was coming from and said it was really up to me what I wanted to do. It didn't really help me in the conversation as I was hoping for an easier or assisted exit, but I had to be firm. I didn't necessarily feel added pressure, but I felt like I had to do more not only to support my mum, but overly support her so she didn't have to worry about anything ever again. So I stayed firm and handed in my notice. The agency that got me the role had put a lot of pressure on me to start on a certain date, and when I came back with the date to the IT Manager he wasn't necessarily pleased about it. Wasn't a no but there was reluctance as my notice would take me up until Wednesday, so the agency wanted me to finish the week before Friday. I really should have had more of my own control at this point but the IT Manager was absolutely right to feel some kind of resistance. The agency was putting even more pressure on me saying, "Well, Dujon, I'm not going to waste my time etc. You'll miss your chance to start the induction with these great architects which you can build a working relationship with. Just tell them that they are a glorified knocking shop. And if they don't let you go previous week Friday you can sue them and get some money." That last bit was under the impression that a one month notice was the same as a 4 week notice but they are quite different; however, he later came back and said he was misinformed. There was no way I could have ever told my current place something like that! So as the days counted on I spoke to the IT Service Delivery Manager as he knew I was leaving. He asked me when I was leaving and I stuck to the date which the agency had said I needed to leave on. He was a bit confused and spoke to the IT Director. After a couple of hours the IT Director called me into a room for a little talk.

"After talking it over with the other guys we've decided to release you on the day you asked for," he said.

This was a huge relief as I was really under it on both ends.

"But just for future reference, it's always better that you finish your full notice whenever you leave somewhere," he added.

I responded, "I understand and I'm sorry. I did say had this been any other situation I would have done so exactly."

But then he said, "Yes but that doesn't really matter as you are employed here" – paraphrasing at this point here. But after the talk we both got up and I was about to leave and then he said "Big Disappointment". That comment was really unwarranted and I wasn't going to respond to it. To be fair, I understand their frustration with me doing what I did, so I just had to take it and move on with it as I was onto a bigger and better role. On my last day none of the managers actually came to London for my last day, but they did ring me to wish me luck as well as the senior IT engineer giving me a final handshake – he was a great person and we ended on great terms. Can only hope that it was all worth it.

CHAPTER 19
– IS THIS THE END?

July 2010, here we go, now the latest greatest adventure begins. First week being for an induction was a great look into what our roles entailed and how the process worked as it was the first time I was to be working as an IT consultant. One of the coolest things I heard was that we were all given an allowance of 2k, which we could use to expense for any type of equipment we needed such as a laptop, phone etc, which was a great motivation for me as this was the first time for me getting something like this where I hadn't paid for everything out of my own pocket – of course this never changed where my exams were concerned. Shortly after we were assigned to people who were called "Career Managers". These were senior consultants who were responsible for you somewhat like a manager but more to manage each individual's goals, so they meet the relevant performance targets for the business. This method intrigued me. It was a very different way of working for me, but I was excited about the aspect, especially with the huge catalogue of IT courses which came with it. Couldn't have been in a better place. One of my first goals was a task I had put on myself which was to obtain my MCSE, as I was only one exam away from completing it.

The following week I passed my final exam and finally achieved the huge certification at 22. At this time Windows Server 2008 exams were out and I was still doing the Server 2003 exams just so I could obtain the foundational grounds of its predecessor before jumping into the latest technologies.

The first few days I was on something called the bench, which was where you were waited to be allocated to a client/project and you spent your time either updating your profile, CV or training. There were quite a few things bubbling around and I couldn't wait to get on doing something. I heard of a project that was available. I spoke to the Architect on that project and got to understand more about what it entailed and it involved a lot of the System Centre technologies I had worked on previously and I wanted that role. What was even better was the office was only at Waterloo which was around the corner from me so was a win-win. I had to wait for a little while to see if that would materialize, which it did but I could only start in about a month's time, so I would have to fill my time doing other things. And this was where the concern I had about the travelling had turned into a reality.

Later that week I got a call from my Career Manager about a couple of days' work engagement in Glasgow.

"Glasgow!?" I said.

"Yes and it's for tomorrow. Book your flight," he responded and that was the end of the conversation.

I didn't even know what the role entailed let alone being told I had to do it tomorrow! I got back in touch with my Career Manager on Skype, who explained what the role was and why the notice was so short. I had been told later that evening so I had no kind of preparation at all. I was under the impression that I could turn down a project if I wanted to. But he explained you can't turn it down as it would look bad on my record. But I still didn't know what I was going to be doing and at this point I had never flown before, and I was going to do it tomorrow with another person I hadn't even met before or had any communication with until that day.

I wasn't happy about it but I thought well this was what I had signed up for knowing this could be the case – though it was definitely more than 50 miles. So I had got my ticket and made my way to Gatwick airport by cab about 6am. And I managed to meet the Architect I was going to be working with and then he explained what my role would be about, which was to shadow him whilst he was doing a discovery phase meeting for a client. It would be an interesting experience, so I thought ok be good to see an architect on this level in action. But the architect turned out to be one of the most difficult guys I had ever met. When we landed at Glasgow Airport he moaned about the luggage I had brought because we had to wait for it in baggage claim and kept making faces, comments and walking around in circles. I wasn't really familiar with how the whole luggage process worked and he knew it was my first time flying but it didn't stop him from going on and on.

We headed straight on to the client site so that the architect could talk to some of the client personnel so he could prepare for the meetings he had for tomorrow and the following day. During this time I was just told and left to sit down at the desk till he got back. Since I didn't have anything to do during this point I used the time to study for my first Windows Server 2008 exam to keep up with my own targets and my own career goals. A short while later he came up behind me and stuck his face right into the laptop like he wanted to be inside it and said, "What are you doing?"

I said that I was just reading the study guide for my next exam. He just looked at me then eventually walked off. Shortly after that we checked into the hotel called the Radisson Blu. Then just under half an hour later he wanted us to go to dinner. He looked at me and said, "Next time, Dujon, change your clothes and take a shower."

What!? I thought. I had never experienced anything like this where anyone would even say anything like that to me. Also, what was funnier was that he only had a backback that wasn't even full so I don't know what change of clothes he had, but that's another story. When we got to the restaurant, he kept looking at me for a minute straight, then he said to me, "Wow you must really get all the girls, don't you with what you do..." It was a real left field comment but I just said like well yeah I have my moments etc.

After dinner he wanted to go for a walk to walk off the food he had eaten, but I didn't realise he was going to walk over a good portion of Glasgow. He walked for a whole hour then we walked back to the hotel so almost 90 mins of walking. I can only assume he would have showered after that like he tried to say to me because I did for damn sure.

Next day was the discovery phase meeting, and was a case of taking all of the technical requirements to formulate a potential design which was for an Exchange implementation. It was interesting to see how it all worked and I did learn a lot from it. As I was told just to sit in and observe, I took notes down of everybody's name and job title alongside some minutes. When we were on a break the architect said to me, just to give advice, normally in these meetings it's good to take note of everyone in the meeting so that we know who everyone is and also what everyone had said.

And I showed him that was exactly what I did. So I had some initiative there on this point although I had to admit that the thickness of the Glaswegian accent did make it tricky for me to record everything but I got there. But overall I did learn a few things on how to conduct a discovery phase and design meeting. A lot more of a relaxed day, we had dinner again just like yesterday which was a lot better than the first time. He asked me if I wanted to go along on his walk but I said I would rather go back to the hotel. But soon as I said that he just walked off and left and went on his walk. I didn't even know where I was. But I've always made sure to keep a track of anywhere I went regardless, not to mention I had Google maps on my phone at the time so I wasn't going to get lost. But I would have thought he would have at least either walked me back or given me some kind of indication of where to go. But I found it anyway.

On the last day we had the final parts of the meeting then we headed back to catch the flight. The plane was quite packed so we had to get a seat wherever we could. Once we landed he gave me a little nod and a thumbs up to check if I was ok. But then as soon as I got off the plane he completely disappeared. I don't know how we got out of the airport that quick and he didn't even say anything to me so I was even more at a loss on how exactly I would have got home. So I ended up calling a cab as that was how I had got there in the first place. Horrific traffic on the M25 at that point.

I was due to start the project in Waterloo the following week and I was able to fill my time on the bench by studying and finishing my first server 2008 exam, as well as doing some design documents for some architects who were working on several different bids. What intrigued me was the massive catalogue of courses which were available, and I was very big into self-development and so I had sent through to my career manager some of the courses which I wanted to do. Later that week I had a catchup call arranged with my career manager and we spoke about them, but he said they had huge costs against them. I was confused. I thought they were owned by the technology giants that made the courses? And I had objectives to do some courses and these were not only mandatory but integral to my role. He also went on to speak about the feedback from the Architect whom I'd accompanied to Glasgow. "He gave you some good feedback and that you showed willingness and initiative. But one thing he did bring up was that you got a cab that cost almost £100?"

I didn't think that would be a negative point as such, considering he had messaged me that same evening when we landed saying, "Oh good thing you got the monorail as I got a cab and it's a lot of traffic." I replied back to him saying I didn't get the monorail, I got a cab too. And that was the end of that conversation. If he was fine to get a cab, then why couldn't I? After all, I was told late in the evening to book my flight and go the next day.

Now I'm starting at the new project. Finally I was going to get some normality at a steady project and I was very excited to get on all of the

System Centre stuff. I had met with two project managers who were running the project from another consultancy working alongside the one I was working for. After a quick rundown of the project I was sat with another consultant who I would be working with as well as having a catch-up with another consultant who was leaving the project for a handover. I had then discovered that there actually was no handover to give as well as no documentation or processes at all, so I had to build everything up from scratch. The role was to document and engineer a process which allowed us to submit design or configuration requests. From what I had been told I was under the impression that this was going to be a technical role doing all of the system centre technologies, but it turned out to be a more documentation process type of role which was not what I signed up for at all. I did tell the career manager but he responded saying I had to do a non-technical role for 18 months. It wasn't the answer or response I was looking for at all. But I had to just accept it and get on with the role. First I had to gather up all the little bits of information I could from the consultant who had left, the consultant I was working with, as well as the project managers.

I had made a note of everything as well as chasing up all of the relevant points of contact within the business and organized meetings so I could create a repository which everyone could see on how this process worked. I built up a relationship with quite a few employees there to the point I was getting bookings to do presentations on how the process worked and relevant points of contacts etc. It was not easy to get everything in place but I did as there was no process beforehand. I had a couple of meetings with one of the project managers who said he really liked everything I was doing so far, so back-to-back positive feedback at this point. I have to admit I really did feel the strain of not doing anything technical at all for a couple of months, and it was even worse watching all the other consultants work on all of the enterprise toolsets whilst I had to gather up a process that wasn't documented. My probation period was coming up but I wasn't concerned about that at all – things were going quite smoothly from what I could see.

I had another meeting lined up with my Career Manager by phone as he was based outside of London and also on another project. He said that he also had a meeting lined up with the project managers so that he could get feedback from them which would help with my profile as well as overall probationary feedback. I was back-to-back in a couple of meetings but I managed to make time for the phone call. So I caught up with the Career Manager.

"I got some feedback, Dujon. And unfortunately it's not good," he said.

"Not good?" I responded. Thinking that can't be possible.

"They said that you've been adding no value and haven't been contributing to the team or project and if he doesn't get his act together we're going to throw him off the project," he said.

I actually thought it was a joke. It really wasn't registering with me.

"That's not possible. I only just had a catchup with the project manager earlier this week and he said I was doing a great job," I said.

"Well I'm not sure about that but that's what they said," he replied.

Now it started to sink in that this wasn't a joke and they really said this. I really wish that was a story where I could actually twist the facts to make it look like I'm the victim, but this was 100% true it wasn't a joke and I went ballistic. I kept telling my Career Manager several times they only just told me a few days ago I was doing a great job! How can I go from a great job to being thrown off the project in a few days!? And if I was doing that badly wouldn't they have said something to me!? I really didn't know what to do but I remember going out into the fire exit stairs, punching and kicking the fire door with blind rage. I couldn't even speak for the rest of the day, I was that furious. It made me think that choosing this role was a huge mistake. Once I got home I spoke to my career manager once again stating that this was unfair and shocking. There's no way I could have got that kind of feedback after being told a few days ago I was doing a great job, that makes no sense.

He responded back saying, "Hi Dujon. I can understand that the feedback was shocking, but he wasn't the only one that expressed this feedback, they all felt the same way." This only made me angrier, and I just felt like the Career Manager didn't even try to resolve the situation or get to the bottom of the fact I had been told something completely different. I asked if I could leave the project voluntarily and he said I couldn't because it would affect feedback, chargeability as well as my probation. But staying here would have only made it worse. I asked him if he could try to get to the bottom of why they said this, and he responded back saying it's difficult for me. I had simply had enough of the conversation at this point.

The next day I went in I wanted some answers from the project manager. He had asked to have a private talk with me so I'm guessing he was already aware I would be confused. He said to me, "I know what you heard must have been really confusing and shocking. The fact is I really like working with you, so we are going to set you with the other project manager to work closely with him on a few things." But out of that meeting I was not told once as to what I did wrong or where I was lacking and an explanation as to why I was told I was going great then terrible in the space of a few days. At this point I didn't want to be part of this any longer. Out of desperation I had messaged the IT Service Delivery Manager at my last role to see if I could return back to my old role.

"Hi Dujon, unfortunately the role has been filled. Hope your role is ok," he responded. I wasn't sure if that was true but I'm actually glad they said this. Why should I have been given a way out and when I was adamant about leaving and taking on this role? This was something I was going to have to sort out on my own. So I started to interview for different roles and I found a great position. But the after-effects of being on a non-technical role showed even more how I was affected technically. My normal self was to ultimately destroy any technical questions or scenarios all the time. But in that interview

I couldn't answer most of them, my mind had literally gone blank. Even certain basics to me I couldn't even get through. I was shocked at how much a non-technical role could have affected me like this. Not long after I had got feedback and of course I didn't get the role. But then a recruiter at the agency said that I should tone my CV down from not being so technical. Now I had really had enough at this point! I was going to have to put my foot down to get off the project.

So I spoke to one of the project managers and raised my concerns on the flippant feedback and the fact it's not technical at all and I wanted off. They took my concerns and started to get the process going. I had another catchup with my Career Manager to explain how I was mis-sold the project thinking it was a technical role and then he started to understand and managed to get the ball rolling so that I could leave and get another placement on a project. Of course, because of everything that had happened they had to extend my probation period to another 3 months as it was inconclusive. But my main victory was that I was getting off.

I started to get a flurry of calls and every call I got was to travel further. One position was to go to Denmark, another in Sweden and then another to the Middle East. As I was no longer going to put up with being placed anywhere I had to speak to the resourcing specialists and let them know I only wanted roles in London or at least somewhere within the 50 mile radius of London.

Whilst I was waiting for placement for another project, a new consultant came on board who was going to be my replacement. We had a few meetings as well as a few conferences with other engineers in Bangalore as they worked closely with me in regards to the process I had engineered and documented. At this point this was the only handover that existed on this project where my role was concerned, so the new consultant would be able to get going right away and he was very impressed with it. We did eventually become somewhat friends and even said that he would write up a letter of recommendation for me as he was aware of the situation I was in and how he came onto the project. Finally somebody actually saw the worth of what I was doing here. He thought the feedback I had got and the extension of my probation period was ridiculous to say the least.

A couple of days later a role came up for a project based in Chancery Lane. So, putting my foot down had really worked and got a chance at a fresh start. And this time it was a technical role! Building a new Windows Server 2008 environment. I had a meeting with the consultant who had put a design together for me to follow and build out. I worked with the project manager on the build out and saw there were a couple of things which couldn't have been done on the design, so we had to make some alterations to the environment. But overall I was finally getting the recognition of my work once again and everything was going smoothly. But it wasn't without its teething problems. For example, once the consultant who did the design came back from holiday he said, "Why does this environment look a little bit different?" and I explained the project manager and I had spotted a couple of things that couldn't have been technically done. I think it was down to the edition of Windows Server which was being used for the scope.

Little did I know the architect who I'd accompanied to Glasgow was also on the project I had a couple of run ins with. I had booked a day off with the project manager. Then when I came back the next day the architect grabbed me and said, "I need to speak to you now. Where were you!? The customer was looking to see where you were." I explained I had booked a day off and had agreed it with the project managers, so I didn't understand the outburst.

"Also I spoke to the consultant who did the design you built out and he said you messed it all up," he replied.

I had explained there were errors in the design, we had to do it differently, in fact I had another Windows specialist look over it and they agreed with me as well so I was protected in that sense. The architect really couldn't have said much more and that was it.

(Self-Motivation Point: Make notes and keep track of absolutely everything. Have everything documented and confirmations of any tasks, changes or alterations by email so you have enough evidence. Sometimes you never know when things can come back at you and for whatever reason it's always best to be protected all round.)

I caught up with my Career Manager once again to explain what just happened and how they were blaming me for things that weren't communicated to them and for things beyond my control. He advised me to show him the communication I had had with the project manager and I did. The architect I went to Glasgow with called me into another meeting again. "There is some work that has to be done in India to perform a handover for this environment, but because you have a problem with travelling we are sending the consultant who did the design instead. But you are causing delays and issues on the project," he said.

What the hell was going on? I'm thinking to myself. I haven't done anything wrong on this project and I got every move I did agreed and checked in black and white as I wasn't going to keep being attacked for things beyond my control. This experience taught me to have evidence upon evidence to ensure no one can keep doing this, so I had done this and let the Architect have it so he could see all my moves and signed off agreements and there was no challenge. At this point I put my Career Manager on alert and let him know the names of the guys who were trying to sabotage me. He didn't necessarily respond back but he had the details because I wasn't going to keep putting up with it.

My probation period was up and it was time to get feedback from my project manager and he gave me a glowing reference. Reflective of everything I was doing, which was brilliant to prove everyone wrong who kept trying to disrupt me. I sent this to my Career Manager and he said that this was great and should complete my probation. I was only meant to be on the role for a month but it got extended to a year. So even better.

I remember one time after work I went to meet up with my Career Manager as he was in town and wanted to give me some congrats as to how well I was doing on my current project. All of a sudden the architect that went with me to Glasgow came to us and they just started hanging together and drinking. I can remember thinking what kind of environment is this? This was the same person I said was trying to sabotage me and blame me for things that were not my fault and they were just laughing and drinking like I hadn't said anything? This really bothered me.

Next phase of the project was to build a SQL failover cluster for the new environment but in the meantime my Career Manager said I needed to expand my profile amongst the internal community so he got me to sign up to a global webinar to do a technical presentation. And at the time I still had a virtual lab and using SCCM (System Center Configuration Manager) 2007 so my presentation was going to be about troubleshooting issues with design, installation and certain admin tasks regarding package deployment etc.

Now I was quite nervous at this point as this was a huge deal to do a presentation this big, but I didn't anticipate it was going to be more than 1000 architects! I could see the number of attendees grow and grow. I had to have been working on SCCM for a minute at this point, but I knew a lot of it. So I had my PowerPoint slides ready for the meeting and whilst I went through the short introduction I had a slight freeze. Really my speech got slower because I was trying to think of what to say at the same time whilst doubting myself, something you see sometimes on Dragons' Den. But then I had a split second thought to just go for it and let go. When you are confident about what you know it should come naturally to just speak, I find when you try to rehearse a speech or pitch, it doesn't come as second nature to you and the moment you think you've forgotten something you have and then you freeze spending time trying to find your place. So I owned the 15 minute space I had breaking down the comparisons between video training and book training, and getting deep into SCCM components. The end result was that everyone wanted to find out where this information could be accessed, which I made public on our intranet.

Once I came out of the meeting room I saw the architect who had given me the technical test over the phone when I interviewed.

"Was that your first presentation?" he asked.

I said yes, replying nervously, thinking I was going to be told how it wasn't that great.

"That was impressive! I could tell you were a bit nervous but that was brilliant!" he said. I was not expecting that at all, and it was just what I needed at this point after all the headaches. The architect who came with me to Glasgow watched the conversation but didn't say anything. He was on the call too so I wondered why he didn't say if it was good or ok or not? But I wasn't going to dwell on it.

One day I came in and I decided to work a bit late to finish off building the SQL Failover cluster as we had a deadline by the end of the week. Something wasn't right this day because I had a bit of a headache so I called it a night about 8-9pm and got a cab back. But the headache I had got bigger and bigger and when I got home it got so bad it made me collapse to the floor in pain. The way to describe it was that it felt like your brain was being pushed against the right side of your skull and it just rested there. I told my mum but she thought it was just a migraine which is exactly what I thought. So I figured sleeping it off would work, but I couldn't sleep on the right hand side due to the throbbing pain I had. I woke up in the middle of night and was vomiting for about 15 minutes, thinking that was the end of it and went back to bed. But it was just the beginning.

I woke up still feeling extremely tired and remembered looking at the bright light thinking it was too bright, it was making my vision funny. So I was opening and closing my eyes a few times thinking this was the case. It turned out I had double vision in my left eye. It was literally pushed to the left hand side and it just wouldn't move.

I told my mum this and she advised we had better go to the doctor's on an emergency appointment. But something more was happening that day. I had this feeling that I had never slept, so I went back to sleep thinking I needed another hour or two. But when I woke up the feeling was stronger. It was like I had never slept in several weeks. I tried to pull myself together because it was getting close to the time I was meant to be in the office so I sent a message to my Career Manager and project manager that I wouldn't be in as I was sick and had to go to the doctor's to get checked out, which they understood.

My mum was trying to keep me awake and was getting frustrated with panic, because she could see that I kept falling the sleep on the spot and her frustration was forcing me to stay awake, as I can imagine her thought process was if I went to sleep I possibly might not wake up. It was almost a comatosing type of sleep. Whilst I had the laptop open, I had gotten a somewhat irate message from the architect who went to Glasgow with me saying "where are you????".

I responded back saying that I had to go to the doctor's to get checked because I was really sick and I had told my Career Manager and project manager. He responded back saying "well thanks for letting the team know". Not that he knew the seriousness of what was going on but it was just the same kind of attitude I had been used to from him, but I was more into trying to keep myself awake.

I went to the doctor's for an emergency appointment. The doctor had advised that I perhaps go to the hospital to get it checked out. His facial expression changed when he was checking me over, so it made me think it may be more serious than I thought. Later that day me and my mum went to the hospital to A&E. We had to wait for about 4 hours before we got seen and I was fighting extremely hard to stay awake. At this point in the day I could barely walk and my sight was seriously impaired and I kept saying let's go home I'll just sleep it off. My mum had to make a noise for me to finally get seen then it was just coincidentally my turn; they kept me in overnight. They did ask me some weird questions asking me if I had AIDS. This only made me more nervous about what could be wrong. They did a CT scan on me later that day as well or some kind of scan as such to see what was wrong. Eventually they got the results and I overheard some of the consultants discussing it and I heard word for word "he has the brain of a 50 year old".

The next morning, the consultant came over to me and my mum and let us know that what I was dealing with was a brain tumour. But it wasn't an ordinary tumour because the blood was in rings which indicated the amount of time it had been there and apparently it had been there for at least 7-10 years. The size was apparently the size of a golf ball. Later on I discovered that the tumour was pressing on the pineal gland which released the melatonin hormone which is released for sleep, which explained why I kept falling asleep. But it also rested on an optic nerve which caused my eye to be pushed so far out impairing my vision. All it made me do was reflect back on some of the headaches I remember having in some of my roles, the sick days caused from them and also a time when I went to play football after work during my time in Chelsea and I physically couldn't move that well at all. I had taken quite a bit of time off during previous role before I started at this consultancy. And to find out all those times I thought I was having a headache, it was the tumour growing bigger and bigger!

I got my mum to ring my Career Manager and explain that I was in hospital and what I was dealing with. Later in the evening after another head scan I was transferred to Kings College Hospital via ambulance. All I can say is an ambulance suspension is damn near like a rally racer!

Once we got there I was greeted by a consultant who said there is a good chance we can give you some radiation treatment to shrink the tumour, which was a relief thinking I wasn't going to undergo surgery. But then the following morning I saw the same consultant and he woke me up to say well because of its size it's going to have to be surgery. Damn. I didn't like it but what I could do at this point? I was going in and out of consciousness, whilst I was fighting to stay awake my mum came but then so did my dad so it just kept re-enforcing how serious this was getting. But at this point I was thinking of so many different things, like awaiting feedback for an interview I had had prior and getting my expenses posted back to my current role. Me not being fully conscious, my attitude was not as worried or focused to the point I had so many injections I didn't care – and I hate injections! But injections mean nothing to me now though. So later that day I was being taken down to surgery but there was a bit of an issue because the consultants promised my parents that they would tell me when I was going to surgery, but they didn't and ended up taking me down early. But I'll never forget when they gave me this form to sign. It basically outlined that as a result of this surgery I could end up permanently blind or dead. This was literally the moment I realised how serious this was, but I was too nonchalant or focused on my interview feedback and expenses to die. I think this is important as I think your spirit plays a big part in surviving anything in general. After a few hours the surgery was done and I was taken to the critical care unit to rest. I remember I got my mum to make sure I got my expenses posted – even though she was extremely stressed I wanted to take her mind off it or keep it occupied by doing this little task. I, on the other hand, was chasing for feedback for an interview I had. My self-motivation had me at a point I was still driven even after recovery. I had a breathing unit and mask on to breathe through all the dried blood I had as well as my vision still being off. I was told during the couple of weeks that I would be on medication for life. Well I suppose it's better than dying, I thought. The surgery had made me seriously weak and I had to get to grips with walking again as I needed assistance to even move around. I pushed myself too far moving around the hospital that when it was the day for me to be discharged I passed out twice. My dad knew this was the day I was getting discharged but he didn't pick me up from hospital and the hospital booked a cab but it left because they kept me waiting for my medication prescriptions so I had to book my own cab for me and my mum. At this point I was confined to the couch with my body going numb on and off and struggling to work and drinking Ribena by the truckload. But I still didn't stop there, I was on the phone and laptop trying to get everyone's Christmas presents as it was only a couple of days before Christmas Day. Once it was

Christmas Day it wasn't exactly a day where everyone felt the joy of me not dying. My dad showed up later not really acknowledging how I was and making comments when I tried to walk saying, "Why is he walking like that? He's walking like he's disabled?"

"He's just had brain surgery and been bedridden," my mum said with a confused face, thinking how could he even say anything like that.

"I'm going to ask questions," he replied whilst turning his head in an opposite direction as he felt he had laid some kind of authority down.

"What questions? You came to the hospital 3 times within the 2 weeks he was hospitalized and asked no questions," she said whilst helping me to walk. This eventually started to get me annoyed throughout the day. At one point he got mad at me because I dropped my phone down the sofa and he kept going on saying "A £700 phone and you turn it on silent! Why would you put it on silent!" He said this whilst searching for it but he took a long time to find it and when we eventually found it he was trying to steal it.

At some point near the end of Christmas Day he decided to start a debate on who was the better parent. But I thought what kind of conversation is this? I've only come out of hospital and it's Christmas Day. He was adamant on saying that he was the reason I'm doing everything I'm doing today, but I had to put a stop to that conversation saying he told me I couldn't even get to this point and throwing the letter away as well as him putting my mother down every chance he got saying he was more intelligent etc. But I wasn't going to put up with this. My vision was still seriously impaired and my head was starting to throb and the last things I said were "I don't like you coming up here putting my mother down when you did nothing to help us and was missing in every checkpoint we ever got to". He got mad and then stormed out. Still very frustrated, I sent him a text the day after he left stating for him not to bother us anymore, we really did not need this after everything we had gone through. He came up later that day enraged almost like he wanted to fight. As I couldn't physically move and with double vision this appeared frightful, but

I didn't care at this point. He was yelling saying, "You're ungrateful! You're ungrateful! What he went through was not life threatening! He's leaning on his illness!".

The last words he said were "You won't see me again". And he hasn't been seen since.

Strange comments considering we were all told if I carried that tumour for a couple more days it would have exploded and I would have bled to death very quickly. It was by some luck that the tumour got so insanely big it seeped out blood slowly so the pressure slightly went down but it was still growing but just not as huge, so it bought me some time to being admitted to hospital for surgery. I had no intentions of dying in my spirit, but would that have reflected reality with the seriousness of what I had, I don't know. But I'm still here.

CHAPTER 20
– ROAD TO RECOVERY

O n the road to a lengthy recovery. I did keep in touch with my Career Manager at my current role and he agreed and advised for me to be off for about 3-4 months. I was trying to be optimistic to a huge level saying I would be back in one month but that certainly was not going to happen.

I spent my time trying to practise walking around again as in my head I was still very weak, and was also getting used to my medication. During this time with regular appointments I was given a pair of glasses which were frosted on the side where my eye was still severely pushed to the side; this would help my eye rest during the time I was resting at home. It almost felt like I didn't have time to rest as I wanted to make sure I held everything down for me and my mum still, so though I was in absolute pain and going in and out of numbness I tried to get myself into my motivated mode. After about a couple of months I went and got back in touch with the owner at the private institute where I'd done the course and he was equally or even more concerned about my current condition, but I was adamant that I was getting better and I wanted to find a new role. After a month of resting I met up with him at the office, but you could see the absolute difference in me. I was wearing a suit but because I had lost so much of the tumour weight (I was about 220+ pounds before surgery and went down to about 150) so I was swimming in the suit as well as the glasses with the one frosted lens. He was quite concerned seeing me like that, but in my mind I had no time to rest, I had to get out there. They managed to sort me an interview, it was obviously the first one just coming out the hospital only a couple of months previously and just getting to grips with walking. I remember one point in the interview they had another interviewer come in who came to greet me and I think they expected me to stand up to shake his hand, but I really didn't have the physical strength. This eventually became the overwhelming bit of the feedback which I received.

Still pushing through I had then connected with a recruitment agent on LinkedIn who had a role for me for a huge IT company again at the familiar side of Liverpool Street. As I did research on the company as well as the role I was so impressed, I had to have this. It may have been the longest and most technically challenging interview processes I had ever seen. I had to go through three different technical test phone interviews. One focused on Microsoft, the other was Citrix and the last one was Virtualization. I had impressed myself, I managed to go through them very well and had decent scores and feedback and was then invited to a face to face interview. I remember there were two roles available and three people (me being one of the three) were at the final stage interview. I did feel some pressure because the last interview I'm sure I visibly looked weak in a duvet type suit and a pair of glasses with a frosted lens. My mum at the time did not approve of any of what I was doing because it was wiping me out working at this rate after surgery, but I had to reassure her I was fine.

What I did next was insane. I attended the face-to-face interview and when I was called up I went and did the entire interview without the glasses! My vision had slightly improved so it wasn't hard-core double vision but still painful to try and see straight ahead. I still believe to this day this was my best interview/performance ever! I had studied and remembered the history of the company and knew all of the board of directors, managers, everybody as well as going through all my healthy experience and further technical quizzing. I swear I came out feeling like I could walk out properly and with 20/20 vision!

I chased the recruitment agent for a few days, anxious for feedback as I knew I had this in the bag, I just knew it. Then on the Friday I got the call. I didn't get the job. I was pretty disappointed and angry and that would have wiped my energy out even further hearing that. The reasoning was because they had perhaps very slightly more experience, but it's crushing to hear that in an opportunity where two roles are available and three people are going for it, I didn't get it. Horrible just horrible. They did say, however, they would definitely take me on in a month or so with no interview needed whatsoever. But after my years of experience in these processes that really didn't mean anything to me. I had heard them all before.

Eventually it was time for me to return back to my current role hoping that things would be a lot better now since my return. I had a conference call meeting with my Career Manager and someone from HR all making sure I was ok health wise. He explained that they had had to extend my probation again because I had got sick and had poor performance last time.

"What poor performance?" I said. "How can my probation be extended again after the feedback I got at the end of my probation and got extended to a year?" I said with confusion. But he explained it's because I didn't finish it and because of the feedback I still had at the previous project. I really didn't like this at all and it only reminded me that I had to get out of here asap.

The HR had made a deal with me that they would cut my work days in half and extend it by an hour every week. I was on a project which would really help me out to get to grips in terms of my energy levels. They had made some things smooth for me as I was still getting paid whilst I was at hospital as well as me getting a big card wishing me to get well. The majority of the names were from the consultants on the project at Waterloo including the project managers that gave me that horrific feedback, as well as some big company managers and directors which was nice to receive.

At this point my eye had pretty much straightened out but I did need those glasses on occasion in order for me get enough rest for me as it was still strained. I had to go and pick up my laptop from the office in Chancery Lane as that's where it last was before I got admitted to hospital. So I made my way there and went into the office and I saw the architect who went with me to Glasgow.

"I didn't think you would be around anymore," he said when he saw me. A very strange thing to say to me and I'm pretty sure he knew what I had just gone through, but I kept it moving to get my laptop which I found was in the new office next to the Old Bailey.

I noticed I was getting emails every week saying they were extending my hours by an hour instead of a month, but I hadn't been placed anywhere yet so I wasn't concerned. The resourcing specialists checked on me and asked me how I was getting on and they promised to only get me roles in London so that I could maintain my hospital and medication appointments.

But the next thing which really put me in a difficult position was when an architect whom I had done some work with before had come to me about a role which would be good for me. But it was in Liverpool!

I said I couldn't do it because I had almost weekly-bi weekly appointments and I was on medication for life. But then another architect joined in saying, "Oh it will be fine, you can get the train back whenever you need to. Also, your Career Manager has also agreed for you to go."

I thought how he could agree for me to take a role without telling me? Especially when I was heavily medication-dependent at this point?

I got in touch with the career manager and he said they had set up an appointment for me at a private doctor's so he could check me out and give me the all clear to go to Liverpool. I thought no way am I doing that! But I was at a point where either I had to leave right now or stick this one out. My mum was like hell no are you doing this! You'd better leave. Even one of the IT engineers at my role in Chelsea told me to just leave, it's only a job at the end of the day and it isn't worth your life. I had gone to meet up with them again about a month after surgery to get practice in walking again so I appreciated the advice. I was doing my best to act like I was fine when I went to visit them, but it was physically challenging.

In the meantime I had managed to get another interview and this was with a small hosting company specializing in cloud technologies. They wanted me to do a presentation for them, and I remembered how much I said I refused these types, but I stuck this one out and I had a presentation ready for the comparisons between Hyper-V and VMWare. As they were based so close to good old Liverpool Street, I was quite amped for this, presentation and all. When I got there and I met the interviewers they were greeting me on their way out, they said that all of the meeting rooms were booked and said if it was ok if we could do the interview at a cafe round the corner which was great for me. But even more, a relief I didn't have to do the presentation! It was quite a relaxed talk about my experience and the projects I had done and more about the role. It was quite hard to read them, to be honest, so I had no clue where I stood or how I felt it went. A homeless guy came up to me after I did the interview asking me if I'd come back from an interview after I gave him a bit of change. I said yes and he said well I'm pretty sure you've got it. I said I hope so!

Back to reality now at my current role, they were still trying to prep me for this role in Liverpool and had one of the consultants take me to Nando's to talk more about the project. I mean the free lunch was great but I was less than enthusiastic about everyone agreeing on my behalf to send me somewhere right after my breakdown of my schedule and getting a private doctor to just give me a once over. But I was more concerned in making sure my mum was good, so I had to do what I had to do. When I got home we both argued about me even considering this and whilst we were arguing I got a phone call. It was the agency representing me for the role I had done the interview for. They said they wanted to see if I had any flexibility on my asking salary. "Ummm...?" I thought thinking this sounds like an offer. He said, "What if I can negotiate down by 2k?" I went with it because I really just wanted to get out of the situation I was in. There was no longer an argument at this point, just anticipation. Then I got another call from the agency saying, "Congratulations, Dujon, you got the job!"

Yes! I was very happy about that, had Bounty Killer and Merciless songs just blasted on loud speaker! But not for too long as my head was still sensitive.

This was the easiest notice I was ever going to give as far as I was concerned, and it was an easy conversation for me and the best part of it was because they kept extending and extending and extending my probation periods my notice period was only a week, so I had a month's rest again!

On my last day I had one final catch-up with my Career Manager next to the new office. I was so stress-free at this point. Once we met up we had a coffee but he opened up with an odd question. "What did you think of the architect you went to Glasgow with?" he said.

"Besides the time we went to Glasgow I never actually really worked with him so I couldn't really comment," I replied. Even though I was stress-free, and I had a new job waiting with no type of travelling, I wasn't going to give anyone the satisfaction of slamming another employee, no matter how much I disliked them – sometimes you have to be very careful what you say and who you say it to. I had all I need which was a new and fresh start and I wasn't going to spoil it by adding negative energy to it.

CHAPTER 21
– REBIRTH OF INDEPENDENCE

A month later, I was now ready to start the new job. It was a very different feel because there was only maybe 12-15 people in the whole company and I was the only person who was going to be looking after the Windows technologies as everyone was an SME for their own dedicated technology group. One thing I did get to do was relax a lot more stress-free here and since I was the SME for all Microsoft technologies, even better.

Anxiety wise my experience with the last role would have brought it on a bit more for me, and even more so because I had not long had surgery so I really didn't want no drama, no hiccups, no nothing. Once I did start, I remember I was given a form, something like an employee form, to fill out for details about myself etc, kind of like an application form. One of the questions on there was if I had any medical issues, injuries, things of that nature. So I felt like I had to put down what I had recently gone through. Once I handed this in, I was called into a meeting room for a meeting with the HR person. "Brain Surgery!?" they said, looking shocked.

I explained about the whole thing and they were very shocked to hear it. It's funny because when I still tell people they are very shocked, horrified, cringe and also look around my head for any scars. I guess I see it very differently because I was so determined to move on and with me not being in a very conscious state I probably wasn't as in tune with what was at stake.

Following on from this I had got on with my role being the Windows SME and analysing the current processes they had with building new machines for new clients, so I took it upon myself to revamp it utilising a tool called MDT (Microsoft Deployment Toolkit) which allowed us to build machines without any user interaction and made our processes quicker. It was a great way for me to add value and stand out. But in the middle of this great initiative, I had set the building alarm off! See, everyone gets given a key fob for the alarm system and if anyone gets in the building first and they open the door the alarm system does a countdown. So one time I got there first and I tried the fob and it wasn't working. Then all of a sudden, the alarm system just went off and it was deadening as well as panicking me. With the surgery I had at the time I was conscious that people would get the impression I was unstable and that worried me even more. So I walked out of the building and across the street and saw another HR person who worked there who said hi to me and said hi back and kept walking. This made it worse because I knew they would be walking into the alarm system going off. After about 10 minutes I went back in and chaos was going on. As they had had issues in the past where a couple of break-ins or attempts had been made, they were nervous about it and they were going to get the police in and check the security systems to see who tried to break in. At this moment I grabbed the HR person I originally spoke to about my surgery and said it was me that did it. I explained I panicked because the fob didn't work and because of the surgery I had I didn't want eyes on me like I was unstable.

The situation did eventually get cleared up, after a short meeting with the IT Manager just letting me know next time just let someone know you did it etc... it looked bad on my part because I saw someone and kept walking so I can only imagine what they would have thought of me then, maybe even now, but I had to get over my past experiences and own up regardless of what I thought people might think. I was also given a replacement fob, but then a few months later down the line I did it again – but this time I waited till someone got in. I felt stupid but it wasn't worse than what I did the last time. Of course this one was my fault as I didn't use the fob correctly but I for damn sure wasn't going to be first in that building ever again!

But besides all that the role was going great, my new machine building system was in place, the latest version of System Centre 2012 was in a beta stage, which I was able to utilise that meant I was able to extend my Windows capabilities a lot further.

I was contacted by Computer Weekly a couple of months into the role and they told me I had been recommended by the private institute I did the course at as a person who would be perfect for an article to be done on me based on my experience with the A+ certification! It was a big deal for me to get any kind of media done on me, so I gladly took them up on this and conducted an interview with the editors. I remember I had said that I completed the exam in about 10 minutes because I was so hyped to do my first exam at 18, but it caused a bit of a debate with the editors about putting it in there as it might have given the impression of the exam being too easy and because CompTIA were also part of the article I could understand. In the midst of this I was working on my next exam, another big task I was taking on and the first after coming back to work from resting from surgery. I managed to pass the exam with flying colours which got me back into the swing of things and I felt like I was back again!

A little while after that the articles were released and they looked great! Being featured in Computer Weekly (magazine and internet) and CompTIA, which had me elated. I remember I was telling a colleague there about it who I became cool with and showed it to them and they really loved it. They even went as far to send it to everyone in the organization saying we have a celebrity in the house.

I did blush a bit because I didn't expect that and I thought it was a great idea. But it came with a backlash which I didn't realise, because the IT Manager had asked to speak to me for a few minutes. He had a small problem with the article. See, in the interview with the editors

I told them where I was working, so what they did was do some research on some of the clients they had and it ended up in the article and the IT Manager said it could be an issue to the clients they had being referenced in this case. I kind of understood, but this was the last reaction I thought would have come from this. But I appreciated the person sending it around anyway.

I did start to have some doubts of my future at the role because it was primarily driven for Linux and software developers and the Windows space was extremely small, almost unnoticeable, so I thought I would investigate the market and see what was out there. I had 3 interviews which I had reached final stages on, I was on top of the world at this point, still liked the feeling of getting these roles and interviewing after the two million no's I received in the past. Then one day I got a random call from an agency in regards to contract roles which I said I wasn't interested about, but we somehow fell into the conversation about contracting and I got to understand a little bit on how that side worked etc. I knew you could get more money from it but I always had the notion, just like a lot of people do in regards to job security and didn't like the uncertainty of being out of a role then looking for one right after – it didn't appeal back in those times, but the model interested me for a bit. My CV at the time was looking like I had an average of 1 year at a perm role due to me wanting to move onto other roles and gain more experience, and with me paying for my own exams and study materials I felt like I had already been a contractor in principal without reaping the higher remuneration benefits. So he said give me a call back if you want to know anything more.

About a week went by and I heard feedback for all of the roles I had. I got none of them! It wasn't necessarily the fact of me coming second this time. But what was strange was the feedback reasoning was odd. One said that he was angry I made it to the final stage without knowing because he didn't like my CV in terms of the duration I had at roles even though I explained the last role I had medical reasons but overall said I was talking BS. I literally laughed at this because it just didn't really make much sense to me. Another one said that "my environment didn't fit theirs"? Still to this day I don't understand it. And the other one I didn't even hear back from at all.

This input a trigger in me, to the motivation which made me now look at the contracting side even more. Because I felt I was working like a contractor anyway, but I also had a possible look into the future that with feedback such as that (or none) what would give you the impression that your role is safe? Why would we assume because we have a permanent role we think it will be permanent? When I worked in Chelsea I witnessed the recession and I saw a sea of desks just empty, it almost looked like the whole company had been fired. So I thought that a contractor would be a lot sharper because they are expecting to not be in a role at some point whereas someone working in a permanent role will automatically assume this is my role for life. A marriage also has the same principles assuming you will be together forever, but it doesn't always pan out that way.

So, I made a call back to the same agency and spoke to the same person as before and I explained that I was ready to look deeper into the contracting game and he gave me the contact of a very experienced contractor, with over a decade of experience. We spoke on emails about how the contract markets were, differences between limited companies & umbrella companies, daily rates and accountants.

I ran with that information and started to do some investigations on my own and the first thing that I could analyse where the demands were on, were skillets! My background had always been an IT Generalist background and therefore my CV was so versatile that I was getting calls for everything! And it had been like that from when I was at Career Legal. But I had started doing a lot more work with System Centre at this particular time and I really got into the private cloud Virtualization side so I decided to expand on this a lot more which made the role more exciting so that the Windows side of the business had more of a say.

In the meantime I was looking at the contracting side a lot more and wanted to get more out of my career and had summed up that there were two options in which I felt was almost like the ceiling of your career. It was to either be part of a consultancy and rise to Architect level, but with my experience at my last job I wasn't about to entertain that idea ever again, so it left me with the other option which was to become a contractor. I was aware of the rates but it wasn't really the main driver. At the same time I didn't really understand how it got broken down also.

I also went onto LinkedIn in my network so that I could analyse current architect profiles and more specifically to those that stuck out and looked impressive enough to have a baseline from. I reached out to a couple who gave me some good material, but I managed to talk to one who gave me such great advice career-wise and contracting-wise. It was a done deal; this was the next step for me to go for. This person's profile was so impressive to me that I could automatically envisage that mine could potentially look like that and with the current press I was getting on my Computer Weekly articles I felt I was in good stead.

Now to discuss the idea with my chain of command, my mother. Her initial reaction to it was "Hell no!" She was totally against the idea and felt it was way too risky, no matter how much it was paying and felt it would be career suicide to attempt it. And I know sometimes I may have ideas on a whim, but this was well thought out and was very similar to the response I faced when I wanted to drop out of college. I had broken it down that the roles I had final interviews for had gone kaput and that I had spoken to so many consultants and architects who gave me great information and I actually had a structured plan. So, after a back and forth for approximately 30 mins (6 hours it works out in argument time) and multiple in-depth questions, she realised that I had everything thought out. She actually recommended that I should speak to the owner of the institute where I did the course to get his opinion on it too.

We met up for lunch and we had a great catch-up, especially now I wasn't swimming in the material of my suit this time.

So we got into the conversation of me getting into the contracting sector.

His reaction was actually much harsher than my mum's was. "It's not a good idea, Dujon, a lot of people go into this side chasing money and it ends up bad for them. Once you become a contractor you won't be able to get back into a perm role. It's like me as I'm the Owner/Director so I could never be looked at as going back to being an employee," he said. It kind of angered me to hear it but I needed to hear that reaction in order to test my dedication and commitment to the idea I had. I went and did the same breakdown I had done with my mum but more technically in depth and he then realized. "You've really done your homework on this, haven't you?" he said. So he actually liked and respected that I was able to come back and provide concrete answers and actual market research to defend why this would work. What he did say was, "Try not to get caught up in the rates. As you are going to be starting out you won't get a very high rate, I would say you would get about £150-£200 a day at the moment." I took it as a challenge as it wasn't the first time I'd heard a cap on my potential salary – back when I did the course and was given a job guarantee contract of £12k - £16k. But the conversation we had overall was brilliant. I had to hear a stronger opinion about what I was planning because if I couldn't survive that conversation or defend it then I would have no chance of pursuing this move.

I had applied for a role on LinkedIn and it was actually the first ever role I applied for on LinkedIn. And they had a role available for a System Center Consultant role which sounded perfect for me, so I went and applied for it. Then I had a phone call and email about a couple of weeks or so after inviting me for an interview but I had no clue who the hell it was! See, I had applied for a few roles in the past which sometimes I don't hear back from then they come back out of the blue, but because I didn't remember the name of the company I had no clue who it was. Then when I looked back I realized oh! This role!

So I managed to set up an interview there and I had a great chat with the IT Manager there. We got on so well and just had a good vibe on the conversation about the technologies and projects there. We were quite like minded because we both were keen to get onto the latest of the latest of technologies, and my role would be to design and implement the entire System Center 2012 R2 suite, which was a massive project for me but I was so down for it you have no idea. He asked me if I had any more questions. I said well I was so excited by the aspect of this project and the company the only question I have for you is when I can start. He laughed.

It ended on a great note. I had a few emails with the HR there as they had called me to set the interview and with my eagerness I pestered them a few times to see if feedback was coming and if it looked good. I was (probably still am) quite impatient when it comes to feedback, I always have been, may not stop for a while to come. Then the following Monday I was just in my room playing some games, about to have dinner and I noticed an email from the HR. I didn't even read it, it said congratulations you got the role! I had never at this point received a job offer like that so that may have been the most amped to get a job offer ever. Only thing was that the role was a "Fixed Term" contract. In other words it's like a short term perm role where the salary is slightly higher but not fully independent type of contractor. But that didn't matter to me because this role was an investment. The opportunity was way bigger than a higher salary. The daily rate was exactly what the owner at the private institute predicted it would be! Well it was slightly more than the top end of what he had said but he was pretty much spot on.

CHAPTER 22
– BEGINNING OF WALSHAM SOLUTIONS

My notice period at the time was 2 months which was crippling for anybody trying to become a contractor.

This was one of the obstacles which I had spoken about with some of my early contractor advisors and they advised to really take the leap. As it was unrealistic anybody would wait for a month let alone 2 months and it did make sense. But I wanted to make everything as failsafe as possible, and I knew there could have been a risk where I got a role offer and had to face a possibility it would be pulled away from me. But I was determined to have a risk-free transition for myself. If need be I would have taken the leap no question, but I had to explore the option of trying to complete this deemed impossible task.

I communicated back to HR that my notice was 8 weeks whilst I was trying to negotiate my notice where I was and it did cause a slight bit of stress, but the HR managed to change my start date on the contract and it just made things so much easier. I could have a smooth change over from perm to contract.

With my clear vision of what I wanted to do it made handing in my notice, knowing I could complete an 8-week notice and start my first contract role was very uplifting for me.

A few more certifications under my belt at this point and becoming a charter member for the first system centre 2012 exams which came out during this time, so I was starting strong. What marked the first day so special was because not far from the office was someone who was throwing computers out of the window because he had failed his HGV licence test and was making huge news at the time.

The project, team and environment was perfect for me. What more motivation can you have when you have a professional size pool table and a regulated fridge full of beer? I had to take advantage of this as quickly as I could. The pool table, that is, as I don't drink and drank even less now that I was on medication. But we really were the dream team especially when I think of times we got requests in and we were being bribed and rewarded with chocolates and Doritos with the chilli dips. Followed by tournaments on the pool table once all checkpoints and deadlines were met. There was one guy I just couldn't beat, I have no idea how he always beat me every time, even when I was ahead with just the black ball left but I guess that's how it goes. Cheating!

Our team morale was very strong as we went to lunches on Fridays all the time which became the infamous Nando's Fridays which everyone goes to now. Does anybody know as to why there is a Nando's next to every train station?

I really got on with the IT Manager there too. As a matter of fact he was the first person I ever heard the phrase "work smarter not harder" from, and that not only stuck with me forever but I use it in my way of thinking all the time. The challenge that I really faced as being a contractor was more temptation, but even more was loyalty. I was getting so much attention now from my CV and especially LinkedIn, it was blowing up full of direct emails from employers, agencies and other direct clients. The phone wouldn't stop ringing, so much so that when I was on a call to tell them I was in a role, another call was incoming, followed by a queue of them. I had been used to being head-hunted for the last 6-7 years but it was getting to a ridiculous amount at this point. And it didn't help they had ridiculous offers being thrown in my face. I wasn't about to leave my role after they had waited a whopping 8 weeks to get me on board. One time I had been contacted for a role with the New York Stock Exchange and the rate was almost double what I was getting. I had the initial phone call with them just to see what the role and project entailed, which seemed pretty interesting. It would have been mad for me to not entertain a first refusal on the role. They had asked to see me for an informal chat with an offer to follow but before I would let it get to that point I had declined to go any further as I explained I had a loyalty to where I was at and I was not going to leave them. The agency said they understood but it didn't stop them from wanting me to just take the role anyway, but I wouldn't budge and they started to throw questions at me saying well why did you apply for this role? I reminded them I didn't as they had contacted me and I had already stated I wasn't going to leave. It was more dealing with the aggression of the contracting market especially when there were roles coming out all over the place.

Another example was when I was contacted for another role which was a project to do with the London Underground, all System Center based projects. They offered me the role right after the call. I was shocked as the rate was even higher than the New York Stock Exchange and the length of the project was for a couple of years. I didn't know what I was going to do about it. Do I leave? Do I turn down an insane offer? Before I could even deliberate on what I was going to do they asked what my notice period was and I said it was 4 weeks, which it was. Then all of a sudden the client went quiet for a couple of days, then I was told they withdrew their offer and gave it to someone else because they could start quicker. This really angered me as I didn't realise that companies could even do things like that – it would have been even worse if I had given in my notice and then that happened!

I took down my CV. And the odd thing was that it wasn't even an up to date CV and I was still getting a stampede of phone calls. I wanted to focus on the role I had at hand as I was still enjoying it and I wasn't going to let the temptation of huge rates just pull me away. If

I responded to every role I had a call for, I'd probably have a thousand roles with a Bible as a CV with one week spent on each. It wasn't a profile that I wanted. During my time there I had started to look at sharing and spreading the knowledge that I had and came across an author who worked for Microsoft and was able to publish blogs/articles on my behalf. So I had developed a three part series which was a comparison of SCCM and MDT in regards to full automation of full life cycle deployment from bare metal machine builds to applications etc. I really liked the feeling of putting these articles and blogs together and to my interest it generated quite a bit of praise.

From my recent success from the articles done on me from CompTIA and Computer Weekly I was contacted again in regards to another article, which was based on success stories of young people who did not attend university – as I had gone straight from College to a private course then a job in about 6-7 months it was something they wanted to focus on. Now I was starting to actually build somewhat of a brand for myself and was starting to get more known in the IT industry in a small way. The bits I enjoyed the most was when I started doing webinar and class appearances at the private institute to show and inspire others that were going through the same journey as when I was 18. At this point I was getting very comfortable in speaking to audiences. Nerves is something that can never be shaken as nerves is what sets the expectation of how you want it to go and the moment you mess up the nerves lock up as a false thinking of failure and then you crumble. As I did many times before, just do it! Reliving some of the experiences I had in the industry at those appearances were interesting and you never fully understand how it sounds to the person hearing it whether it gives them any hope, if it's inspiring enough...

The biggest challenge I would face is when I was approached for another role, a very huge role and this was for the Foreign Commonwealth Office (FCO) based in Wolverton. The project was immensely huge and involved a design of the whole System Center suite just like my current role but there was some cloud technologies to also integrate with. I still was somewhat reluctant to entertain it as it was so far, and with the complications I had where my medication was concerned I felt it would be too much to take on. But knowing me I knew I was going to go down there and entertain the madness. It was the first I had ever seen of a building that was so secure that your mobile phone signal was cut off the moment you even approached the building in the techno park. I had to also lock my phone away on stepping into the rest of the structure. Top notch security I would imagine. After the informal chat they showed and introduced me to other contractors who were also travelling quite far distances. Some lived in Manchester and Liverpool and had to stay in the area just to work down there! Not sure if that was a commitment that I could fulfil, to be honest. Shortly after that meeting (same day in fact) I was offered the role and was the biggest rate out of any role I was offered at this time. They even went and offered me slightly more than what I had asked for. To set the scene I was only 24 and the rate...let's just say it was at the high rate of 2019! I talked to a couple of friends I had and they said, "Dujon, for that money I'd walk barefoot to get there!" So everyone was for it then!

But part of me still couldn't do it. I still really enjoyed the role I was in and not to mention to monitor my hospital appointments and medication as well as travelling that far out with the possibility of living down there was too much to take on. They tried to offer me as much flexibility as possible but even my own doctor advised against the idea of doing this. Though I could have had my medication transferred over there if I decided to live down there, but my appointments were too fresh and aggressive at this point. For the sake of my own health and the loyalty I had, I had to make the right decision (which feels like crap btw) and I let the role go. It stayed on my mind for quite a while. Not necessarily depression but it did affect me for a little bit, but that's how I knew I had done the right thing. One time in the office, we were all working quietly in the office all minding our business and we heard a couple of staff from the developer team round the back of us and all of us blindsided. Round the back there were a lot of spare machines and servers, and they needed one or two spare servers. In the midst of this happening...all of a sudden we heard

"Bend Over!"

"Bend Over!"

"Bend...Over!"

We were all looking at each other laughing. Then all of sudden the unexpected came. Whoever was back there said

"Bend Over!"

"Ahhhhhhhh yeeeaaaahhhh that's it!"

We were dying of laughter, we couldn't breathe at this point! I laughed so hard I had an excruciating headache. The developer guys had come round the corner to see what all the laughing was about, but of course they wouldn't have known how it sounded when we can't see anything and we overheard the loud conversation such as the one they were having. Eventually they got why it was funny and how it sounded, but you really had to be there to see it. That may be the funniest moment I've ever seen in all my career! That and the time when Meek Mill - Dreams and Nightmares came on randomly during their music playlist after they were playing all kinds of pop music. It was funnier when everyone was saying "What the hell is this!?" Got even funnier when the IT Manager came in and said the same thing!

I'd got over the role I let go, and during this time the 6 month contract had lapsed so I and the IT Manager had a conversation about it. He said that I could have either a 3 month extension, or even join as permanent. Now becoming permanent interested me because I was already on a fixed term contract which is kind of in-between and I really liked where I was at and managed to negotiate a good salary from it and it was announced then and there I was now a perm member of the team. I was happy about this: we had the dream team there. Then another member of the team who was also on a fixed term contract also went perm too! So now we were all solidified!

One guy that I remembered in our team always gave us laughs, but one thing I had really taken notice of was that he never took lunch. I mean ever! He worked so hard every day he was the most loyal desktop support person I saw, he walked the floors every day to ensure everyone was good with no issues, but he never took time out for himself at all. The heart of our lunch Fridays or any days in fact may have been just so that we could not only eat and bond as a team but also so the desktop support guy would get a break too. Me and the other guy who also went perm at the same time picked up on the same thing; he also mentioned he had never placed a bet before either, on top of never really going to lunch. So we took it upon ourselves to take him to a betting shop so he could get the experience. There was no cashing in on beginner's luck on this one as the horse lost. But still. Another thing about him was that he loved fish and chips. There are a lot of people that like and love fish and chips, but he was ritualistic about it to the point if there were no mushy peas he wouldn't eat it. And if they gave him normal peas they had better mush them up! He liked going through the tasks of removing all of the batter from the fish before he would eat it too...but at least he was going out to eat.

With all of the contract roles I had been sent my way, some were not fully over as one agency got in touch with me in regards to a contract role which I did try to shake off until I eventually found out it was for a university. This was something quite personal for me due to the fact that I had skipped university and went straight into a job/career and I had missed out on that part in life. It was such a gap between me and my other friends because whilst I was working at 18, they were still in college. By the time I was 20 they would have been at university. And by the time I was working at the IT consultancy they would have probably finished university so it's like an entire lifetime I missed in that aspect. So to be able to experience that atmosphere and kind of see what it would be like, I had to go for it.

Rate-wise it wasn't as high as the other offers I had but that didn't matter to me. This was potentially to be my first real contract role, and at first I was more toying with the idea of using an Umbrella Company as it seemed so much simpler. But I did more digging and had a look at the structure of a Limited Company and at first it looked like an overwhelming amount of information. When you let information overwhelm you it can cloud your judgement as to which can be the better options for you. So, when I looked into it, I understood the process of registering to Companies House, VAT registration and getting an account for tax affairs and how it broke down the daily rate, which if done right would be significantly more than an umbrella company. So this jumped at me and I thought OK I'll stick with this approach as I wanted the proper self-employed experience.

So it was interview day, and I had been sent to the wrong building. But it was ok, the right one was down the street and I finally got there still in the nick of time. I didn't really get a chance to observe the campuses as I was focused on the task at hand. I was interviewed by four people so I knew I was going to be prepared for a technical grilling all around from architects and managers. The IT Manager there was a woman and I had only come across one before so this was cool to see. When I first met her and we sat down I was like wow! You're going to have to forgive me, I'm a young man at this point in time! All I can say is that she gave me an extra lift of confidence in that whole interview. I did kind of want to impress her so and it turned out to be one of or possibly my best interview. Not necessarily just doing great on the technical grilling but more the overall competency based questions and conversations. I thought to myself leaving the interview, I know I've got this, I have to get this. To be able to see what the Uni life would have been like, I just needed it. Back end of the week I got the call to say I had got the job! It was a wrap from there; I was going to be a full contractor now! My current role was one of the best places and people I worked with, so it was going to be hard to leave, but this was something I had to do. I explained to the IT manager the opportunity I had and he understood it was during the time I was still on the "fixed term" part of the contract so he gave me time to think about it. After sitting on it for a few days I let them know that taking the new role was the right thing to do.

One of my last tasks with the team was to help to move office down to Moorgate, so at least I got to see where they are now before I left. But everything I worked for from 18 led me up to this point of being somewhat at the top of my game. To be a full independent contractor at a university. Ready to start a completely different chapter in my career, the only way is up!

EPILOGUE

The Struggle Continues

The story never ends, the journey never stops and the history continues to write itself. Sometimes the greatest thing about when you make history is that you're not aware you are making it.

The process of always bettering yourself, stepping up your game and to keep focus is not just an action and not a chore, it's a way of life. Your brand will always be your brand regardless of what position you may hold, whether it's a cleaner or a CEO. You are the leader in your domain. The only time you can become a follower or just an employee is when you choose to.

Looking back on my journey I see and achieve things I didn't expect to. At least I didn't expect to so quickly. I had always felt that something great would happen, but it would never just come to me if I just waited for it. Sometimes I feel like I got to where I got to too easily, or maybe it's because I enjoyed the journey.

There will be many after me that may have the same thinking as I did when I was eighteen years of age, to take an opportunity and own it regardless of what ridicule and doubt they may face. The journey is enjoyable but not without its struggles, its headaches and challenges and they never stop. The struggle will always continue but you have to be in love with the struggle.

For all the ones at eighteen that choose to enter the IT industry and start from this age or to take advantage of any opportunity at any age, I hope this book can guide on what you will expect to see and what to watch out for to help you along your journey. I think what was so fascinating about mine was that I didn't know of anyone who did this before me, so there was no book or manual on how to achieve what I achieved, but just me and my mother to march through the snow. With all the knowledge I've obtained over the years I have to share it, you're wrong for not sharing your knowledge and experience with others. I want people to surpass me in what I did by great, huge, humongous levels past me.

I also say, one of the best currencies we have is time. What can be achieved in 24 hours is amazing if you applied your goals or task to it. And one of the biggest flaws we sometimes have is the ability to read a book, gain information, gain ideas, gain knowledge...and then we do nothing with it. As I have said in this book, you can gain knowledge and motivation from anywhere...and the biggest role model at the end of the day is you.

Reality of Self-Motivation

When I wrote this I thought "Self-motivation is simply the form of"... and then I thought, you know, this is not what we are going to do. I cannot simply start off my first time effort with a cliché about what self-motivation is and how it's going to help. To be perfectly honest I've never read or sat through an entire speech of any motivational speaker.

Why, you ask? Because you cannot teach motivation. Motivation in my opinion requires some kind of focus and you have to be in an action or doing it before you can even be motivated. Thought provokes motivation and that's really the idea of what motivation is.

I'm hoping I didn't just contradict myself by saying I won't go into a cliché and then end it with one.

But I will go somewhat into my interpretation of what self-motivation is in its rawest form.

Many people have tons of motivations but they happen to either have weak foundations or volatile dreams. So for example let's take the biggest one, which is money. Everyone wants to be rich (assuming by money) and no one wants to work, not even me to be honest. If I could be rich and didn't have to work then this book wouldn't even see the light of day, or wasting battery on the Samsung Galaxy S9 to type this.

Another example of what keeps people motivated is family, loved ones, children etc.

While they do seem like very normal and understandable motivations, in the long run they are weak. If you are solely motivated by money then you will become a slave to it. And will do anything for that motivation which makes your vice a drug motivated by another drug. Many disasters and bad decisions normally come from just being motivated by remuneration benefits. How much money do you need? We say well it's never enough well when the hell is it enough? Do you need enough to buy the world ten times over? It's a very vague and blind like motivation which will only end in tears.

And the harsh reality is that being motivated by family has the same pitfalls. You can never predict how your family may turn out in the future or if relationships will strengthen, weaken or stand the test of pressurized times. But as much as we have people that depend on us, it's always the closest to you that will hurt you the most. Your family can know your kitchen very well so it's very easy to grab a knife and stab you in the back. Your motivation shouldn't just have a dependency, because when that dependency is compromised then where is your motivation after that?

You have to remember that whilst we have the mentality of 'I'm doing this for my family', you have to take into consideration that they would feel the same about you (they should at least). So if you are destroying yourself to support them then you are hurting them at the same time; don't assume they would rather you kill yourself or break your neck just to help them as they would rather see you in wealth of health and with communication of this can join everyone together as a single unit all helping each other. Now that is what I would call no other self-motivation better than that, a family that can stick together.

We need more to push ourselves, and this is where self-motivation comes in. Because the person you should be motivated by is YOU.

You are the only person that can achieve what you want to achieve and you have to understand to love yourself enough to be motivated. If you don't love yourself or are motivated for yourself then how can you pass this on?

I don't necessarily consider myself intelligent or smart, I never had any special abilities to use to my advantage or special schooling, so I have to believe (in fact know) that if I can make it then anybody can.

It's really about finding the motivation you already have, as opposed to falsely creating one or building around a dependency which is already a given in terms of adult responsibility.

My experiences may have depicted words of a harsh reality of Self-Motivation, but motivation can be a mixture of pleasure and also pain, to unlock your true inner-self and you have to love yourself enough to be self-motivated.

Time...